Around About Woking

10th Edition

Produced entirely by volunteers of
the Woking branch of the National Childbirth Trust,
Charity Registration Number 801395

The National Childbirth Trust (NCT) offers support in pregnancy, childbirth and early parenthood. We aim to give every parent the chance to make informed choices. We try to make sure that all our services, activities and membership are fully accessible to everyone.

NCT Enquiry Line: 0870 444 8707
(8:30am to 5pm Monday to Thursday, 8:30 am to 4pm Fridays)
www.nctpregnancyandbabycare.com

Produced by the Woking branch of the National Childbirth Trust
Registered Office:
Alexandra House,
Oldham Terrace,
London, W3 6NH
Registered no. 2370573
Registered charity no. 801395

This tenth edition of *Around About Woking* published 2004.

ISBN 0-9522797-2-X

Printed and bound by EntaPrint, Cranleigh, Surrey

Illustrations by Andy Hamilton at Elephant Shoes Ink Ltd.

Published and distributed by:
NCT Woking Branch
c/o Alexandra House
Oldham Terrace
London
W3 6NH

PROJECT TEAM

The following team members worked together over an 18-month period to plan, research and produce this new updated edition, each taking on specific roles, as well as supporting other team members with their activities:

Eve Peyton
Project Leader and Advertising Co-ordinator

Su Blackburn
Art Editor

Alexa Gardner
Project Accountant

Karin Quinn
Administrator

Julia Barnes
Printing and Publishing Co-ordinator

Louise Carroll
Research Co-ordinator

Lisa McLaren
Desktop Publisher

Carol Sharman
Marketing, Publicity & Sales Co-ordinator

The Around About Woking Project Team would like to thank the following people for all their help in producing the book: Katie Arnold, Sophia Atkins, Linda Barber, Charlie, Hector and Fergus Barnes, Suzanne Beattie-Jones, Kath Brown, Kate Bruton, Steve and Phoebe Carroll, Ally Edwards, Catherine Fortescue, Holly Gardner-Hall, Louise and Alan Gosling, Tim Hall, Andy Hamilton, Roz Haynes, Deborah and Joshua Howard, Fiona Howells, Amanda Karki, Susan Lewis, Nicki Mantel-Cooper, John and Jake Martin, Kathryn McCormick, Janet Pelham, Dan and Emily Peyton, Helen Powell, Brian and Katie Quinn, Jonathan and Charlotte Richards, Nicola Roberts, Sheila Saul, Andy and Holly Sharman, Tracey Sheldrake, Janine Townley-Lewis, Mel and Chris Watson, Jackie Weller, Helen Wellman and the NCT Woking Branch Committee.

Advertising

Please mention Around About Woking when contacting any of the services or advertisers listed in this book. To advertise in future editions of this book or the NCT newsletters, please contact Around About Woking, NCT Woking Branch, c/o Alexandra House, Oldham Terrace, London, W3 6NH, phone 07050 801057 or email aroundaboutwoking@hotmail.com.

Disclaimer

The information contained in this book was compiled from original research undertaken in the months immediately prior to publication. All information is believed correct at the time of printing. Nevertheless, the publisher can accept no responsibility for errors, omissions or changes in the details given. The views expressed in this publication are not necessarily those of the National Childbirth Trust or the publisher. Over time information will change and readers are strongly advised to contact the venues/providers directly for the most up-to-date opening times and prices. The appearance of an advertisement in this book does not imply endorsement of the company or its products by the NCT, nor does it constitute a recommendation. If any errors or omissions are discovered, please write to Around About Woking, NCT Woking Branch, c/o Alexandra House, Oldham Terrace, London, W3 6NH or email aroundaboutwoking@hotmail.com.

All proceeds from the sale of this book will go towards funding NCT specialist workers in the Woking area.

SYMBOLS

£ cost of main course is £5 or less

££ cost of main course is £5-£12

£££ cost of main course is more than £12

toilet facilities including disabled

toilet facilties

baby changing facilities

private area for breast feeding

public facilities for warming food or milk

access to the facility for pushchairs

access to the facility for double buggies

access to the facility for wheelchairs

P free parking at facility

outdoor play area

indoor play area

creche available

toys sold

shoes sold

books sold

clothes sold

bicycles sold

CONTENTS

INTRODUCTION

WELCOME TO the tenth edition of Around About Woking, a guide book for parents and carers of pre school children in the Woking area. We hope this book will become an invaluable source of information and help you make the most of the opportunities that Woking has to offer. The team that produced this book are mothers with babies and small children who live in and around Woking and have themselves found the previous edition of the book extremely useful. Whether you need a restaurant with highchairs, information about ballet classes, details of childcare options, or somewhere to go for a special day out, we have done our best to include it all. We've introduced a couple of innovations to this edition to make the guide easier to use. We've used symbols to denote certain facilities to help you to see at a glance what is available and help you plan your trip accordingly. We've also included internet and email addresses as they are so much a part of everyone's lives today.

This book is published by the Woking branch of the NCT and all profits from its sale will go to them to help fund the many services it provides. Launched in 1957, the National Childbirth Trust aims to help parents enjoy all aspects of parenthood. It offers ante-natal classes, help lines and educational events, not to mention all the social opportunities of meeting and making new friends both during pregnancy and after. It also publishes books on all aspects of childcare, holds Nearly New Sales and gives parents a chance to meet others going through the same experiences they are. The Woking branch of the NCT has a full social diary that all carers and parents of babies and pre-school children are welcome to participate in. Information on the various services offered by the Woking branch of the NCT along with contact details is contained in the advertisements throughout this book.

We have all had a lot of fun putting this book together. Everyone who has worked on this project has done so on a voluntary basis, pooling our talents and giving up valuable free time. We hope that you have fun using it too. We took a decision not to include personal views on individual entries but to try to keep them objective as everyone has their own preferences and requirements. We have tried to make it as

(continued)

comprehensive as possible but if we have missed anything out please forgive us and if there is something you think we should include in the next edition then email us at aroundaboutwoking@hotmail.com.

Finally, the last word must go to our children. They have given us all a new perspective on life. They have eaten more biscuits during our Monday meetings than we thought humanly possible. Without them, however, we would not have had the opportunity or the incentive to compile this book. We have looked at the place we live with fresh eyes and have sometimes been surprised at the variety and diversity of things to do and places to go. We very much hope you enjoy using this copy of Around About Woking.

Local activities for parents & children

KEEPING YOUR CHILDREN occupied is a task that will take up increasing amounts of your time so we've devoted a considerable amount of effort to this chapter in order to give you as wide a choice of activities as possible.

The activities listed in this chapter range from those for parents with babies, such as mother and toddler groups, which are a great way to meet other parents as well as offering your child a chance to begin to build their own social circle; through to activities that they will start when they are older and may continue for many years, such as riding, dance classes or martial arts. We've included post natal exercise classes in this chapter as many of us find that after the birth of a child we want to do something to get back into shape as well as details about public leisure amenities which offer something for all the family.

Many of the classes and activities must be pre-booked and some may have to be paid for in advance so you should always call beforehand to check availability, particularly as some may have waiting lists. Most of the toddler groups are run on a 'turn up on the day' basis. but it's always a good idea to check before your first visit just to avoid disappointment.

BABY AND TODDLER GROUPS

All Baby and Toddler Groups are suitable from birth to school age unless otherwise stated.

Bethany Babes

St Mary of Bethany Church
Mount Hermon Road
Woking
Surrey GU22 7UH
01483 723424

■ *Mon 10:00-11:30, 14:00-15:30, Tue 10:00-11:30, Wed 10:00-11:30 term-time only*
■ *£1 voluntary contribution*

Safe baby area, sit and ride toys, slide, tunnel, books, puzzles, crafts and singing sessions. Waiting list may apply. P

Bisley Parent and Toddler Group

Bisley Village Hall
School Lane
Bisley
Surrey GU24 9EG

■ *Wed 09:30-11:30*
■ *£1.50 per family paid half-termly*

Range of toys including sit and ride toys, slide, see-saw, trampoline, play kitchen, farm, garage, dolls, books, baby toys and train set. Craft activity, story and singing session each week. Refreshments provided. Waiting list applies. P

Brookwood Babies and Toddlers (BATS)

Large Memorial Hall
Connaught Road
Brookwood
Woking
Surrey GU24 0AL
Jane Griffiths 01483 826471 or 07880 933562
gareth.jane@virgin.net

■ *Mon 09:30-12:00*
■ *£1.50 per family*

Large hall offering separate sit-and-ride area. Facilities include baby area, books, pop-up play area, dressing-up clothes, home corner, car mat and cars as well as a wooden slide and climbing frame. Musical instruments and a singing session as well as a craft activity organised every week. Video rental available. Cost includes tea, coffee, squash and biscuits. Turn up and play. P

Bumps and Babes at The Mustard Tree

Mustard Tree Coffee Shop
New Life Church
High Street
Old Woking
Surrey GU22 9ER
Emma Rainier 01483 770177
Mandy Dicksee 01276 476928

■ *Mon 10:30-12:00 (First and third of each mth)*
■ *£1*

Toys available for babies up to toddling stage (about 18mths), while expectant and new parents can chat and have refreshments. Call beforehand or seeNCT newsletter for dates. Turn up and play. P

Bumps and Babes at The Vyne

The Vyne Centre
Broadway
Knaphill
Woking
Surrey GU21 2SP
Mags McLaren 01483 480745

■ *Thu 10:00-12:00 (last of each mth)*
■ *£2 suggested contribution*

NATIONAL CHILDBIRTH TRUST

Membership

As a charity, the NCT relies on income from subscriptions to continue its work. Woking NCT members receive a free quarterly newsletter and access to the virtual coffee mornings as well as the national magazine, New Generation. Use the application form in this book, call the Woking Branch on 07050 801057 or to pay by credit card call the Membership Hotline 0870 990 8040

www.nctpregnancyandbabycare.com

Toys available for babies up to toddling stage (about 18mths), while expectant and new parents can relax, chat and have refreshments. Call beforehand or see NCT newsletter for dates. Turn up and play.

P

Byfleet Toddler Group

St Mary's Church Hall
Rectory Lane
Byfleet
Surrey KT14 7LL
Kim Daymond 01932 400436

■ *Fri 09:30-11:00 term-time only*
■ *£1 for first child, £0.50 each additional child. First visit is free*

Climbing frame with slide, home corner, train set, trampolines and craft table. Baby corner with bouncy chairs and push-along toys. Summer outings, theatre trips once a year and nights out for mums also arranged. Refreshments for children included. Waiting list may apply.

P

Cheery Cherubs

Large Memorial Hall
Connaught Road
Brookwood
Woking
Surrey GU24 0AL
Hilary Newland 01483 487319
Claire Unthank 01483 486122
hilary@cooksgreen.freeserve.co.uk

■ *Thu 09:45-11:30*
■ *£1.50 per session*

Climbing frame, craft table, pop-up tents, small bikes, soft play area for babies and singing at end of session. Refreshments provided. Turn up and play. P

Chobham Mother and Toddlers

St Lawrence Church Hall
High Street
Chobham
Surrey GU24 8AA
Lyn Porter 01276 858541

■ *Thu 09:45-11:30*
■ *approx £2 depending on age and number of children*

Separate baby area, also pregnant mums welcome. Craft activity, variety of toys focusing on "activity" play, singing at end. Refreshments provided. Opportunities available for joining parenting and other related courses. Turn up and play.

The Coign Church Mums and Toddlers

The Coign Church
Church Street West
Woking
Surrey GU21 6DJ
01483 714150
www.coign.org

■ *Tue and Wed 10:00-11:30*
■ *Free–voluntary contribution of biscuits!*

Informal play session with range of toys including tunnels, slide, trampoline, sit and ride toys, craft table, home corner, singing at end. Refreshments provided. Waiting list may apply.

Emmanuel Chapel Toddlers

Emmanuel Chapel
18-20 Portugal Road
Maybury
Woking
Surrey GU21 5JE
Sally Levett 01932 346484
Suzanne Smith 01483 755689

■ *Fri 09:30-12:00 term-time only*
■ *Voluntary contribution only*

Sit and ride toys, slide, Duplo, painting, baby toys, art, craft and singing sessions. Turn up and play.

Holy Trinity Toddler Group

Holy Trinity Church Hall
Chobham Road
Knaphill
Woking
Surrey GU21 2SY
Jenny Clarke 01483 475483

■ *Thu 13:30-15:00 term-time only*
■ *£1 per family or £5 per half term*

Informal play, with sit and ride toys, craft table, story and singing. Separate baby area. First week free. Quiet (but not private) areas available for breastfeeding. Opportunities available for joining parenting and other related courses. Waiting list may apply.

Horsell Evangelical Church Mother and Toddler Group

Horsell Evangelical Church Hall
High Street
Horsell
Woking
Surrey GU21 4SS
Phyllis Croucher 01483 829880
Gwen Childs 01483 771901

■ *Thu 09:30-11:00 term-time only*
■ *£8 per family per term, refreshments extra*

Age range from birth-3yrs. Safe area for babies. Slide, trucks, climbing equipment, playhouse, books, puzzles, craft activities and singing session. Library available to parents. Regular attendants of the church have automatic entry to the group. Waiting list may apply.

Knaphill Baptist Church Mums and Toddlers

Knaphill Baptist Church
High Street
Knaphill
Woking
Surrey GU21 2PZ
01483 831408

■ *Tue 09:45-11:45 term-time only*
■ *£7.50 per term per family*

Activities include craftwork, dressing-up clothes, various toys, books and puzzles. Singing sessions with piano accompaniment. Extra sessions are run during Summer holidays. Occasional book and Tupperware sales. Waiting list may apply.

Knaphill Methodist Church Parent and Toddler Group

Broadway
Knaphill
Woking
Surrey GU21 2DR
01483 472524 (ask for contact details for Tina Neoptolemos or Kelly Cranfield)

■ *Wed 10:00-12:00*
■ *£1.50 per family*

Informal play with range of toys including craft activities and singing session. Refreshments provided. Parking at rear of Co-op. (Due to redevelopment, group temporarily based in Knaphill Scout HQ, Waterers Rise, Knaphill, GU21 2HU to Dec 2004.) Turn up and play.
P

Little Adventurers

Church of the Good Shepherd
Coldharbour Lane
Pyrford
Woking
Surrey GU22 8SP
Jackie Miller 01932 349558
www.wisleywithpyrford.org

■ *Wed 14:15-15:15 (First and third of each month)*
■ *Free*

Songs and storytime, crafts and informal play, with a Christian theme. Refreshments provided. Turn up and play. P

Little Lambs

The Church Hall
Send Evangelical Church
Send Road
Send
Woking
Surrey GU23 7AD
Aleida Hawkins 01483 473396 (Tue)
Debbie Hurdle 01483 223255 (Fri)

■ *Tue 10:00-11:30, Fri 10:00-11:30*
■ *£0.60 per family*

Age range from birth-3 yrs. Separate baby area, various activities including sandpit, playhouse, book corner, play dough, ball-pit, sit and ride toys, craft activities and singing session. Refreshments provided. Waiting list may apply. P

Little Monkeys

Joan Robinson Hall
The Maybury Centre
Board School Road
Maybury
Woking
Surrey GU21 5HD
Catherine Okon 01483 762982
Katrina Vujovic 01483 841701

■ *Tue 10:00-11:30 term-time only*
■ *£1.50 per family*

Age range from birth to 3yrs. Separate baby area, various activites including craft table, singing session, parachute games. Refreshments provided. Turn up and play. P

Little Seeds

The New Life Church Hall
The New Life Church
High Street
Old Woking
Surrey GU22 9ER
Pauline Mills 01483 747473

■ *Thu 10:00-11:30*
■ *£1 per family*

Age range from birth-3yrs. Safe area for babies. Activities include sand, painting, play dough, wooden railway as well as story time, singing session and parachute games. Hall is upstairs, pram and pushchair park downstairs. Waiting list may apply.

Our Lady Help of Christians Mother and Toddler Group

Our Lady Help of Christians Roman Catholic Church
Madeira Road
West Byfleet
Surrey KT14 6DH
Carolina Sher 01932 340180

■ *Wed 10:30–12:00 term-time only*
■ *£0.20 per week*

Informal play session, with toys and play dough. Refreshments provided for parents. Parking is Pay and Display on street. Turn up and play.

Pram Club

St John's Church Hall
Camphill Road
West Byfleet
Surrey KT14 6EH
Joyce Ebbage 01932 346471

■ *Wed 14:15-16:00*
■ *£1 per family*

Safe play area with a range of activities, toys and singing session. Refreshments for parents. Turn up and play. P

Pyrford Mother and Toddler Group

Arbor Youth Club
Teggs Lane
Pyrford
Woking
Surrey GU22 8ST
Julia Haygreen 01932 887215

■ *Thu 10:15-11:45*
■ *£1 per family*

Baby area with suitable toys. Craft activities, toys, books, puzzles, playhouse, Christmas party, books and card sellers. Self-service kitchen for refreshments. Turn up and play.

Rainbows Mother and Toddler Group

St Michael's Church
Dartmouth Avenue
Sheerwater
Woking
Surrey GU21 5PJ
Michele Walley or Norah Hubbard
01932 341694

■ *Thu 10:00-12:00 term-time only*
■ *£0.80 per session plus £0.10 for each additional child*

Sit-and-ride toys, activity toys, playhouse, craft activities, see-saw and slide. Music played and refreshments included in cost. Turn up and play.

Sparks

St Peter's Church Centre
Church Street
Old Woking
Surrey GU22 9JF
Pauline Wilde 01483 722098

■ *Wed 10:00-11:30*
■ *£0.50 per family*

Separate room for babies. Craft sessions alternate weeks, sit and ride toys, play dough, puzzles, books,

singing session. Limited parking on site, but free car park nearby.

St Andrew's Parent and Toddler Group

St Andrew's Church
Denton Way
Goldsworth Park
Woking
Surrey GU21 3LG
Rev Christine Harrison 01483 723879
www.goldsworthpark.org.uk
standrews@goldsworthpark.org.uk

■ *Mon 10:00-11:30*
■ *£1.70 per session*

Age range from birth-3 yrs. Slide, sit and ride toys, activity toys, baby toys, craft and singing sessions. Turn up and play.

St Andrew's Toddler Group

St Andrew's United Reformed Church
White Rose Lane
Woking
Surrey GU22 7HA
Marianne Basey 01483 714216

■ *Wed 10:00-11:30*
■ *£0.50 per family*

Informal play session, with sit and ride toys, playhouse, playdough, puzzles. Separate baby area with toys. Refreshment provided. Turn up and play.

St J

St John's Church
Youth Group Hall
Church Path
St Johns
Woking
Surrey GU21 7QN

Karen Wilcock 01483 858868

■ *Wed 09:30-11:30*

■ *£1.50 per session*

Craft activities, storytime, songs and music as well as various toys for informal play. Snack time with juice and biscuits provided. Turn up and play.

St Mark's Tots

St Mark's Church
Westfield Road
Woking
Surrey GU22 9NG
Lyn Boyman 01483 715603

■ *Tue 10:00-11:30*

■ *£0.50 per family*

Various toys for informal play, craft session, storytime and singing session. Refreshments provided. Waiting list may apply.

St Mary's Mother and Toddler Group

St Andrew's Room
St Mary the Virgin Church Hall
Church Hill
Horsell
Woking
Surrey GU21 4QQ
Alison Prince 01483 768806

■ *Tue 10:00-12:00*

■ *£0.50 per session*

Variety of toys for informal play. No craft or singing activities organised. Tea, coffee, juice and biscuits provided. Turn up and play.

St Paul's Church Mother and Toddler Group

St Paul's Church Hall
Oriental Road
Woking
Surrey GU22 7BD
Linda Mayne 01483 771717

■ *Tue 10:00-11:45*

■ *£1 per session*

Variety of toys for all ages, singing session with guitar. Drinks and biscuits provided. Turn up and play.

Sunbeams Christ Church Baby and Toddler Group

Christ Church
Town Square
Woking
Surrey GU21 6YG
Janice Vickers 01483 740873 ext 8
www.ccwoking.org.uk

■ *Wed 10:00-11:45 term-time only*

■ *£1 per session per family*

Separate baby area. Wide range of toys for all ages including slide, play dough, wooden railway, water play, kitchen and playhouse. Song and story time at end of each session. Opportunities available for joining parenting and other related courses. Parking available in the town centre car parks. Turn up and play.

Trinity Toddlers

Trinity Methodist Church
Brewery Road
Horsell
Woking
Surrey GU21 4LH
Liz Robbings 01483 825763

■ *Fri 10:00-11:45*

■ *£1.50 per session*

Safe area for babies, wide range of toys including climbing equipment, craft activities, quiet/reading room and end of session songs. Summer and Christmas parties organised. Drinks and biscuits provided for children, tea, coffee and cake for carers. Opportunities available for joining parenting and other related courses. Free parking is limited. Waiting list may apply.

West End Childminders

Sports Pavilion
Benner Lane
West End
Woking
Surrey GU24 9JP
Lesley Tweedie 01276 858939

- *Wed 09:30-12:00*
- *£1 per child per session*

Group for childminders and nannies to meet. Various toys available for informal play. Waiting list may apply.

West End Toddlers

Sports Pavilion
Benner Lane
West End
Woking
Surrey GU24 9JP
Carol Rooney 07739 040541

- *Tue 09:15-11:30 term-time only*
- *£1 per week per family. First session free*

Age range from 6mths to 3yrs. Range of toys available for free play as well as structured activities such as reading and singing sessions. Turn up and play.

Woking Registered Childminding Group

Trinity Methodist Church
Brewery Road
Horsell
Woking
Surrey GU21 4LH
Fiona Howell 01483 772454

- *Wed 10:00-11:45 (every second of mth)*
- *Cost covered by annual fee*

Toddler group for registered childminders, with separate baby area, craft activities and storytime. Drinks provided. Waiting list may apply.

Woking Twins Club – Toddler Group

St Michael's Church Hall
Dartmouth Avenue
Sheerwater
Woking
Surrey GU21 5PJ
Outi Ellesmere 01932 354963

- *Mon 09:30–11:30 all year except Bank Holidays*
- *£2 per family for non-members of the Twins Club, free to members*

Toddler group open to all families with twins or multiple births. Turn up and play.

Woodham Mother and Toddler Group

Church Hall
All Saints Church
564 Woodham Lane
Woking
Surrey GU21 5SH
Frances Embury 01483 769157
Elaine Evans 01932 347348

- *Tue 10:00-11:45*
- *£1 per family per week*

Large hall with wide selection of toys including toy kitchen and tunnels. Various craft or puzzle activities each week. Separate baby area with box of baby toys. Singing session at end. Waiting list may apply.

QUICK REFERENCE GUIDE TO TODDLER GROUPS

Monday

AM - Bethany Babes - Mount Hermon, Brookwood Babies & Toddlers, Bumps & Babes - Old Woking, St Andrew's - Goldsworth Park, Woking Twins Club - Sheerwater.
PM - Bethany Babes - Mount Hermon.

Tuesday

AM - Bethany Babes - Mount Hermon, The Coign Church - Woking, Knaphill Baptist Church, Little Lambs - Send, Little Monkeys - Maybury, St Mark's - Westfield, St Mary's Church - Horsell, St Paul's Church - Maybury, West End Toddlers, Woodham All Saints - Woodham Lane.

Wednesday

AM - Bethany Babes - Mount Hermon, Bisley, The Coign Church - Woking, Knaphill Methodist Church, Little Adventurers - Pyrford, Our Lady Help of Christians - West Byfleet, Sparks - Old Woking, St Andrew's - Woking, St J - St John's, St Peter's - Old Woking, Sunbeams - Woking, West End Childminders, Woking Registered Childminding Group - Horsell.
PM - Pram Club - West Byfleet.

Thursday

AM - Bumps and Babes - Knaphill, Cheery Cherubs - Brookwood, St Lawrence's - Chobham, Horsell Evangelical Church, Little Seeds - Old Woking, Pyrford, Rainbows - Sheerwater.
PM - Holy Trinity - Knaphill.

Friday

AM - Byfleet Toddlers, Emmanuel Chapel - Maybury, Little Lambs - Send, Trinity Toddlers - Horsell.

CLASSES, CLUBS AND ACTIVITIES – BABY

Baby Massage
Chris Woollatt
3 Ashley Close
Walton-on-Thames
Surrey KT12 1BJ
01932 223918

■ *Mon, Thu and Fri at various times*
■ *£20 per course of 4 sessions*

Lessons in baby massage along with some baby yoga, for infants over 6 weeks but not yet crawling. Weekend sessions can be arranged if partners would like to attend.

Baby Massage
Fiona Hughes
01483 287750
grant@fiona29.freeserve.co.uk

■ *Days and times by arrangement*
■ *£25 for a one-to-one session, group rates available*

Lessons in baby massage which aim to develop a 5 minute routine that can easily be slotted into your day. Lessons held at instructor's house. Maternity reflexology and pre and post natal massage also offered. Playroom for older children available.

Baby Massage
Ele King
07930 540931

■ *Evenings and weekends only, days and times by arrangement*
■ *£20 per group session of 5 babies or less, larger groups of up to 10 babies are £5 per baby, one-to-one sessions £15.*

Lessons in baby massage for infants over 6 weeks. Instructor travels to parents' house.

Baby Massage
Monique Harrison
07900 827619

■ *Days and times by arrangement*
■ *£10 per person per session for groups of up to 8 babies*

Lessons in baby massage and reflexology for infants over 6 weeks. Instructor travels to parents' house. Maternity massage also offered.

Baby Signing
Georgia Askew
Mytchett Canal Centre
01252 520133
www.babysigning.co.uk
georgia@babysigning.co.uk

■ *Thu (occasionally Tue instead) 10:30-11:30 term-time only*
■ *£4 per child for each weekly class and £10 per adult for the introductory session*

Introductory session for small groups of carers lasting approximately 90 minutes, held at venue of group's choice. Weekly classes at Mytchett Canal Centre for 6mths-2 yrs, lasting 45 minutes. Classes consist of teaching component, singing and stories followed by a chance to chat and exchange tips with other signing families over a cup of coffee. No need to book.

Baby Yoga
Swami Satvikananda
Ottershaw Brook Hall
Brox Road
Ottershaw
Surrey KT16 0GH
01932 872587

■ *Tue 10:30–11:30*
■ *£6 per lesson or £30 for 6 consecutive lessons*

Baby yoga classes that combine exercise with songs to give parents confidence in handling their baby and encourage suppleness and relaxation in baby. Babies can start yoga from as young as 2 days and continue through to toddler age.

Tinytalk UK – Merrow

The Jeffries Hall, St Pius' Church
Laustan Close
Horseshoe Lane
Merrow
Guildford
Surrey GU1 2TS
01483 577729
www.tinytalkuk.com

- *Fri 9:30–10:30 and 11:00–12:00 term- time only*
- *£4 per lesson per family*

Signing and singing classes for parents and children from birth-2yrs. Parent and child learn a number of signs for useful everyday words and phrases. Classes include elements of fun with singing of nursery rhymes and action songs. Toys available for children to play with while parents relax with a coffee. Lessons last 30 minutes. No need to book.

Tinytalk UK – Send

The Lancaster Hall
Send Road
Send
Woking
Surrey GU23 7EZ
01372 842934
www.tinytalkuk.com

- *Wed 13:30–14:30 term-time only*
- *£4 per lesson per family*

Signing and singing classes for parents and children from birth-2yrs. Parent and child learn a number of signs for useful everyday words and phrases.

Classes include elements of fun with singing of nursery rhymes and action songs. Toys available for children to play with while parents relax with a coffee. Lessons last 30 minutes. No need to book.

CLASSES, CLUBS AND ACTIVITIES – CRAFT

Ceramics Café

High Street
Ripley
Woking
Surrey GU23 6BB
01483 224477
www.ceramicscafe.com
ceramics.cafe@virgin.net

■ *Tue–Sat 10:00–18:00, Sun 11:00–18:00 (also some late night openings)*
■ *£2 per decoration plus cost of item(s) £5-£15*

Baby hand and foot prints on tiles and plates, etc. Paint your own ceramics for 4yrs and upwards. Parties catered for, party pack costs £10 per child. Parking opposite in sports ground.

Paint Train

Milford Village Hall
Portsmouth Road
Milford
Surrey GU7 5DS
01483 458791
www.paint-train.co.uk
info@paint-train.co.uk

■ *Tue 10:00–11:15*
■ *£2.50 for under 2yrs and £4.50 for over 2yrs*

Arts and crafts sessions for 1–5yrs, activities include painting, pasting, modelling and making cards. Refreshments served and art materials for sale. **P**

CLASSES, CLUBS AND ACTIVITIES – DANCE

Active Education

St Andrew's Church Hall
Goldsworth Park
Woking
01344 622154
jtennison@hurstlodgesch.co.uk

■ *Mon, Tue, Thu and Fri*
■ *Cost depends on age and class*

Dance classes in ballet, tap, modern and jazz for 2½ yrs upwards. Parking limited to those with very young children, older ones must be dropped off.

Gillespie School of Irish Dancing

St Dunstan's Church Hall
Woking
01932 857217
lorraine@lgillespie.fsbusiness.co.uk

■ *Tue 15:30-16:30*
■ *£3 per class plus a registration fee of £12*

Irish dance classes for 4yrs upwards. Younger children are 'buddied' up with older ones to help them gain confidence and get involved. Classes payable in advance per half term. Parking in Heathside car park nearby.

Harmony Dance

Ockham Village Hall and Horsley Village Hall
01483 222041

■ *Thu and Sat*
■ *Cost depends on age and class*

Dance classes in ballet, tap and modern jazz for 2½ yrs upwards. Classes payable in advance per term. **P**

Kelalou Academy of Irish Dancing

Old Woking Community Centre
01483 858283
kelalou.academy@tiscali.com

■ *Mon 16:00–17:00*
■ *£4 per class*

Irish Dance beginners classes for 3yrs upwards. First month on pay-as-you-go basis, thereafter classes payable in advance per half-term. Classes held in upstairs hall.

Paula Waite School of Theatre Arts

Valley End Hall, Bisley Village Hall and Winston Churchill School
01276 856621

■ *Mon-Sat*
■ *Cost depends on age and class*

Classes in ballet, modern and tap, limbering and free work, street jazz, group and private singing and drama. Ballet from 2yrs upwards. Pupils can be entered for exams and festivals. Classes payable in advance per term.

Pirbright Ballet School

Lord Pirbright's Hall and St Saviour's Hall, Brookwood
01276 709393

■ *Mon, Tue, Thu and Fri*
■ *Cost depends on age and class*

Classes in ballet, modern and tap. Ballet from $2^1/_2$ yrs upwards, tap from 5yrs. Pupils can be entered for exams. Two free trial lessons offered before being required to book for a term. Classes payable in advance per term.

Rosina Wenham School of Ballet

St John's Memorial Hall, Goldsworth School and Pyrford Village Hall
01483 827204
claire.hern@ntlworld.com

■ *Mon–Sat*
■ *£35-£50 per 10 week term depending on age and class*

Dance classes in ballet, tap and modern jazz. Pupils can be entered for exams and take part in shows and festivals. Ballet for $2^1/_2$ yrs upwards, tap and modern from 5yrs. Waiting list may apply.

Silke Mackay School of Dancing

Holy Trinity Church Hall
Chobham Road
Knaphill
Woking
Surrey GU21 2SY
01483 764489 or 01252 689393

■ *Tue pm*
■ *£38 per term*

Ballet classes for $2^1/_2$ yrs upwards.

Susan Robinson School of Ballet

Byfleet Methodist Church, Greenfield School, Woking and United Reform Church, Woking
01932 342238
balletbyfleet@aol.com

■ *Mon–Sat*
■ *Cost depends on age and class*

Dance classes in ballet, tap and free jazz from 3yrs upwards. Pupils can be entered for exams and competitions. Classes are payable in advance per term. Note, not all facilities are available at all venues.

Woking Arts Management

Jenny Lowde 01483 770893

Offers advice on performing and visual arts and music for all ages. Also offers classes and can put you in touch with arts tutors, schools and classes.

CLASSES, CLUBS AND ACTIVITIES – GYM AND FITNESS

The 1 – 6 Gym Club

Several venues – East Horsley, West Horsley, Merrow and Guildford on various days, ring for details
01483 284744

■ *£6 per lesson, reduced to £5 for second child*

Gym activity classes for 8mths–6yrs, structured according to age group. Each class has a maximum of 12 children with 2 instructors. Start with ball ponds and softplay, progressing through to B.A.G.A awards for the 4½-6yr olds. Classes lasts 45 minutes. Free trial lesson offered before booking. Must be booked in advance.

Ice Pups Skating Classes

Guildford Spectrum
01483 443322
info@guildfordspectrum.co.uk

■ *From £48.50 for a 10 week term*

Ice skating classes for 3–5yrs. Skate hire and helmets are included in fee. Waiting list may apply. See main Spectrum entry for facilities.

Kindergym

Woking Gymnastics Club
Kingfield Road
Woking
Surrey GU22 9AA
01483 771426
www.woking-gymnastics.ukf.net
info@woking-gymnastics.ukf.net

■ *Mon–Fri 09:30–15:30, 40 separate classes*

■ *£4.95 per session plus £7.50 annual membership*

Structured gymnastics sessions for 12mths-5yrs with parental participation on specialised pre-school equipment, run by fully qualified B.G.A coaches. Each session lasts 45 minutes. Playpen with toys available for younger siblings. Waiting list may apply. **P**

Martial Arts Classes

Sleeping Storm Dojo
Hook Road
Epsom
Surrey KT19 8TU
01372 749458
www.sleepingstorm.com
fightback@sleepingstorm.com

■ *Fri pm*

■ *£5 per session, pay-as-you-go basis for first 4-5 sessions, then payable monthly in advance by standing order.*

General martial arts training for 3–5yrs as an introduction to judo or karate. Children learn the basics of etiquette, punches, kicks and break falling, helps build confidence and improve health and fitness. Staff to child ratio 1:10. **P**

Tae Kwon-Do Classes

HED TKD
PO Box 3398
Wokingham
Berkshire RG41 2XJ
07740 100841
www.hedtkd.co.uk

■ *Mon and Wed pm, Sat am Winston Churchill School, Woking*
Mon and Wed pm Brooklands College, Weybridge
Tue and Fri pm Guildford County School

■ *Cost varies according to age and level*

Classes in Tae Kwon-Do from 3yrs upwards. Training improves basic motor skills and concentration, helps instil confidence, respect and discipline. Classes take place all year round and children can join at any time.

Tot's Tennis

Woking Lawn Tennis Club
Pine Road
Woking
Surrey GU22 0DX
01483 765715
mark@mgleisure.com

■ *Tue 13:30, Fri 13:30 and 14:15*
■ *£4 for members, £5 for non-members per lesson paid in advance for term of 8 lessons*

Tennis skills for 3–4 yr olds, using games to teach hand/eye co-ordination, catching, throwing and hitting of balls. Lessons are outdoors so running shoes required. Lessons last for 45 minutes.

Tots Trampoline

UniSport
The Sports Centre,
University of Surrey
Guildford,
Surrey GU2 7XH
01483 689201
www.unisport.co.uk
s.edie@surrey.ac.uk

■ *Fri 11:00*
■ *£2.50 per session*

Located in the Sports Centre on the University campus (just off the A3), these unstructured sessions revolve around 2 full-size trampolines but also have beams to walk on, footballs and lots of toys. Suitable from birth–4yrs. Children are encouraged to learn safety skills while enjoying themselves, parents must supervise at all times. Parking permits must be obtained from the Sports Centre reception. Sessions last for 1 hour.

Tumbletots Woking

Laker's Youth Centre
Denton Way
Goldsworth Park
Woking
Surrey GU21 3LG
01372 273649
www.tumbletots.com

■ *Wed am, Fri all day various times depending on age group*
■ *£4.50 per class plus £17 membership per year*

Physical activity classes for 6mths–7yrs, part of national active play/gymnastic programme for children, based around music, action songs and rhymes. Parental participation required up to 3yrs. Classes arranged by age group, Gymbabes caters for 0–12mths, Tumbletots walking to 5yrs and Gymbobs for 5–7yrs. Fees include insurance and T-shirt. Each session lasts 45 minutes.

Tumbletots Weybridge

01932 564512
www.tumbletots.com

■ *Tue am Byfleet, Wed and Fri am Addlestone*
■ *£4.50 per class plus £17 membership per year*

Physical activity classes for 6mths–7yrs, part of national active play/gymnastic programme for children, based around music, action songs and rhymes. Parental participation required up to 3yrs. Classes arranged by age group, Gymbabes caters for 0–12mths, Tumbletots walking to 5yrs and Gymbobs for 5–7yrs. Fees include insurance and T-shirt. Each session lasts 45 minutes.

CLASSES, CLUBS AND ACTIVITIES - MUSIC

Jack in the Box

01483 202740

■ *Tue and Wed am Yehudi Menuhin School, Cobham*
Fri am Albury (south of Guildford)

■ *£63 for course of 12 plus £10 joining fee*

Pre-school music group for $1-3\frac{1}{2}$yr olds, with emphasis on fun with music. Features music specially written for this age group, CD included as part of package. All classes taught by musical experts and make use of props, pictures and percussion instruments. Free trial session offered.

Jambaluka Music and Movement Workshops

01252 620279

www.jambaluka.co.uk

jambaluka@hotmail.com

■ *Mon am Mayford Centre, Wed am Guildford Spectrum, Thu am Staines, Thu pm and Fri am Woking Leisure Centre*

■ *Cost varies according to venue (average £5 per session)*

Developmental musical workshops for 5mths-5yr olds. Actions to music, circle songs, knee bouncers, puppet shows, percussion instruments, maypoles, parachutes and other props and visual aids. Mayford Centre does not have a lift and there are stairs up to hall. Note, not all facilities are available at all venues. Parties can be catered for.

Jo Jingles

Woodpeckers
Castle Road
Horsell
Woking
Surrey GU21 4ET
01483 850310 or 07785 997309

■ *Mon–Fri various times and locations in the Woking area*

■ *Approx £4 per class*

Structured music and movement sessions for 1–5yr olds, sessions lasting 45 minutes. Singing and movement using percussion instruments, action songs and rhythm games. Courses payable in advance for each half-term.

Kindermusik

Westfield School
Bonsey Lane
Old Woking
Surrey GU22 9PR
01784 469461

sca.west@surreycc.gov.uk

■ *Mon am during term-time*

■ *£26 per term*

Music, movement and games with instruments for 6mths-5yr olds. Each class lasts 30 minutes.

Kindermusik

Chobham Pavilion
01276 62407
www.musicwithvanessa.com
vanessa@musicwithvanessa.com

■ *Thu am*
■ *Cost varies according to age (around £4.50 per session) plus £27.50 for a home pack*

Music and movement program for children, focusing on whole child development with home pack for continuation of activities outside of classes. Classes for 0-15mths include some baby signing and baby massage as well as musical activities. Separate classes for 15mths-3yr olds. Each class lasts 45 minutes.

Music Funtime

Church of the Good Shepherd
Coldharbour Lane
Pyrford
Woking
Surrey GU22 8SP
01932 349380 or 01932 400485

■ *Mon 10:30 and 11:30, Wed 09:30, Fri 09:30 and 10:30 term-time only*
■ *£14 for 5 weeks, discounts available for siblings*

Fun but structured learning to music, using song, pictures, rhythm sticks and other percussion, movement, shapes and colour, from 6mths-5yrs. Younger siblings can attend from birth.

Music Monsters

Horsell
01483 721473
www.musicmonsters.co.uk
pauline@musicmonsters.co.uk

■ *Mon 9:30 and 10:30*
■ *£3.75 per class or £3.15 per class if you pay in advance for a half term*

Musical workshops ffrom 9mths-5yrs, each class lasting 45 minutes. Singing, dancing, listening to music, playing percussion instruments and joining in with stories. Classes held in teachers home so no double buggy access.

Music with Mummy

01483 833780 or 01483 835464
www.musicwithmummy.co.uk
lesley.worrall@ntlworld.com

■ *Thu and Fri, am and pm*
■ *£3.50 per class, payment in advance per half term*

Structured music session for 1-3yr olds with original songs involving percussion instruments, action and fun. Classes held in teacher's home so no wheelchair access.

Stepping Stones

01784 45347

■ *Tue pm Jurgen Centre (Englefield Green)*
Wed pm Staines Methodist Church

■ *Approx £3.30 per class but varies according to age*

Music classes for 2-8yr olds, inspired by philosophies and methods of Kodaly, Jaques-Dalcroze and Geza Szilvay. Parking in Pay and Display for Staines venue. **P**

Under 5's Jives

07973 421941 or 01483 476011
andreacottage@hotmail.com

■ *Fri 10:00 and 11:00 Chobham Pavilion*

■ *£28 per block of 7 classes, £21 for second child*

Music class for 1–3yr olds, consisting of nursery rhymes, songs with actions, musical instruments and parachute games. Other props used are finger puppets, bubbles and a beach ball. Aims to enhance development through music, rhythm, use of new language, actions and use of social skills. **P**

CLASSES, CLUBS AND ACTIVITIES – RIDING

Fenns Farm Riding and Livery Centre

Fenns Lane
West End
Surrey GU24 9QF
01483 797349

■ *Mon–Sun afternoons and evenings, all day during school holidays*

■ *£10 per group lesson and £21 per private lesson*

Lead rein lessons, activity days, walkabouts, hacking and gymkhana for 3yrs upwards. Lessons last 30 minutes. **P**

Pat Barnes Riding Stables

Shey Copse
Old Woking Road
Woking
Surrey GU22 8HS
01483 721708

■ *Tue–Sun*

■ *£15 per group lesson at weekends, £14.50 during the week*

Lead rein lessons with hats provided for 4yr olds upwards. Lessons last 30 minutes. **P**

Pots Trots

Higher Park Farm Equestrian Centre
Halebourne Lane
West End
Surrey GU24 8FL
01276 856335
www.higherpark.co.uk

■ *Mon–Sat 08:00–20:00, Sun 08:00–13:00*
■ *£13 per lesson*
Lessons involving games for 2–5yr olds. Children learn to ride with a peer group, parents leave the children for duration of 30 minutes lesson.

Walkabout
Cliff Hatch Stables
Saunders Lane
Mayford
Woking
Surrey GU22 0NU
01483 747028
denisepassant@aol.com
■ *Mon–Sun 09:00–17:00*
■ *£8 plus £0.50 hire charge per 30 minute session*
Shetland ponies for hire, children sit on ponies and are walked around grounds under control of parents. Suitable for 18mths upwards. Lessons offered from 5yrs. Facilities for birthday parties available.

CLASSES, CLUBS AND ACTIVITIES – SOFT PLAY

Fizzy Kids
10 Camp Road
North Camp
Farnborough
Hampshire GU14 6EW
01252 669977
www.fizzykids.co.uk
info@fizzykids.co.uk
■ *Mon-Sat 09:30-18:30, Sun and Bank Holidays 10:30-17:00*
■ *£1.00 under 1yr, £3.25 under 4 yrs, £3.95 over 4yrs*
Rope bridges, tube slides, tunnels and huge ball pool. Separate area for under 4yrs with slide, ball pool, trikes, see-saw and trampoline. Cafe serving drinks, sandwiches and paninis. Children's portions and baby food available. Parties catered for. Free parking a short walk away at Napier Gardens Centre.

House of Play
Big Apple
Crown Square
Woking
Surrey GU22 6HR
01483 727100
■ *Mon–Sun 10:00–18:00*
■ *£2.75-£3.25 under 5yrs, £3.50-£3.95 over 5yrs, depending on times and days*
Recently refurbished padded baby area, soft ball areas, trampolines, wendy house, little tables and chairs with umbrellas. Height restriction applies up to 9/10yrs.

Pick 'n' Mix Playstore
Woking Leisure Centre
Woking Park
Kingfield Road
Woking
Surrey GU22 9BA
01483 771122
■ *Mon–Fri 10:00–18:30, Sat–Sun 09:30–12:30*
■ *£2.70 under 4yrs and £3.70 over 4yrs*
Three storeys of soft play for under 12yrs with ball pools, ropes, swings, slides and tunnels. Separate area for younger children. Parties catered for.

Roker's Little Angel's Playworld
Fairlands Farm
Aldershot Road
Guildford
Surrey GU3 3PB
01483 236667

■ *Mon–Sun 09:30–18:30*
■ *£2.50-£4.50 depending on age and time of visit*
Indoor adventure soft playground for under 11yrs with ball pools, ropes, swings, slides and tunnels. Separate area for under 4yrs. Parties catered for. Café serves hot and cold meals and has highchairs.
P

Specky's Pirate Ship

Guildford Spectrum
Parkway
Guildford
Surrey GU1 1UP
01483 443322
www.guildfordspectrum.co.uk
info@guildfordspectrum.co.uk

■ *Mon–Sun 09:30-17:00*
■ *£3 per child, additional child £2.50*
Four storeys of soft play including ball pools, trampoline, bungee run, tube slide, cargo net, sky glide and interactive spooky cave. Parties catered for.
P

Toad Hall

Goldwater Lodge
Goldsworth Park
Woking
Surrey GU21 3RT
01483 799700

■ *Mon–Sun 10:00-18:00*
■ *Free until child can walk, £2 if walking and under 2yrs, £3.25 2–4yrs and £4.25 5yrs and over*
Three storey indoor softplay centre for babies from birth–11yrs with ropes, slides, ball pools, soft shapes and bikes. Restrictions on the amount of time allowed on equipment in school holidays. P

CLASSES, CLUBS AND ACTIVITIES – SWIMMING

Aqua School

01483 306964
www.aquaschool.co.uk
lyane@aquaschool.co.uk

■ *Mon Chertsey, Godalming and Guildford, term-time only*
■ *£90 for a 10 week course*
Swimming lessons for 3mths–4$^{1}/_{2}$yrs. Emphasis is on water play to build up confidence. Classes encourage babies to swim underwater. Underwater photos offered. P

Baby Swimming

80 Spencer Crescent
Oxford
OX4 4SW
01865 771397
www.babyswimming.co.uk

■ *Mon–Sun various times. Venues at Guildford, Leatherhead, Walton, Farnborough and Crowthorne*
■ *£94 for a 10 week course*
Swimming lessons teaching underwater method for 3mths–3yrs. Throughout the first 10 week course, babies will begin to learn to swim by themselves underwater. Premises are accessible to pushchairs and wheelchairs but due to space restrictions pushchairs cannot be left in the premises. P

Arena Leisure Centre - Swimming Lessons

Camberley
Junior Courses Office - 01276 27755

■ *Mon–Sun various times*
■ *Approx £40 per course*
Swimming lessons from 4mths upwards, 10 week courses throughout

the year. NCT swimming classes also held at the centre. See main entry under Sports and Leisure Centres for full details of amenities.

Coral Reef – Bracknells Waterworld - Swimming Lessons

■ *Mon–Sat various times*

Swimming lessons from 6mths–4yrs during term-time. Can be booked over the phone. See main entry under Sports and Leisure Centres for full details of amenities.

Guildford Spectrum - Swimming Lessons

General program open to children of 4yrs and over. See main entry under Sports and Leisure Centres for full details of amenities.

Guildford Spectrum - Duckling Swim Club

■ *Thu and Fri 12:00*

■ *£14 per term*

Fun swimming session for $1^{1}/_{2}$ hours without instruction, but under instructor supervision. Toys and armbands available. See main entry under Sports and Leisure Centres for full details of amenities.

Guildford Spectrum - NCT Swimming Lessons

■ *Tue 13:30–15:00*

See main entry under Sports and Leisure Centres for full details of amenities.

Woking Pool in the Park - NCT Swimming Lessons

■ *Mon 15:00, 15:30 term-time only Wed 13:30, 15:00 term-time only*

■ *£3 per lesson plus £10 registration fee per term*

Swimming lessons for 0–5yr olds, held in the training pool, aimed at getting children used to the water, using nursery rhymes, songs and play. Lessons last for 30 minutes. Non NCT members welcome. See main entry under Sports and Leisure Centres for full details of amenities.

Woking Pool in the Park - Swimming Lessons

■ *Mon-Sat various times, term-time only*

■ *Approx £50*

Swimming lessons from 6mths upwards. Centre operates 164 swimming courses for children each week on various days and times. See main entry under Sports and Leisure Centres for full details of amenities.

CLASSES, CLUBS AND ACTIVITIES – MISCELLANEOUS

Ambassadors

The Peacocks
Woking
Surrey GU21 6GQ
01483 545855
www.theambassadors.com/woking

■ *Cinema £4 child, £5 adult during the day. Theatre prices vary*

Theatre and cinema complex shared by New Victoria Theatre, Rhoda McGraw Theatre and Ambassadors Cinema. Theatre occasionally stages productions suitable for young children. Cinema shows children's films every Saturday and Sunday morning. Parking in town centre public car parks.

Arabic Language Course

Shah Jehan Mosque
149 Oriental Road
Woking
Surrey GU22 7BA
Rahat Nadeem 01932 400207

■ *Fri 15:45-16:30*

■ *£10 per half-term plus £10 registration (discounts for siblings)*

Spoken language classes for 3yrs upwards, using fun techniques such as games, puzzles and picture books. There is provision for nappy changing, but soiled nappies must be removed from Mosque. P

Early Learning Centre Playtime

15 Commercial Way
Woking
Surrey GU21 6XR
01483 755751

■ *Tue 9:30–11:30*

■ *Free*

Free weekly session to allow children to play test the toys in store. Suitable from birth-8yrs. Parking in town centre public car parks.

Fun-Centred Activities for Children

Shah Jehan Mosque
149 Oriental Road
Woking
Surrey GU22 7BA
Lucy Bushell-Matthews 01483 825769

■ *Tue 15:45-16:30*

■ *£10 per half-term plus £10 registration (discounts for siblings)*

Islamic education for children aged $2^1/_2$-10yrs, based around story telling, songs and puzzles for the younger children. There is provision for nappy changing, but soiled nappies must be removed from Mosque. **P**

La Jolie Ronde

01483 870789 or 01483 473688

■ *Mon–Fri after school*

■ *£3 per session*

Fun French classes for 4–10yrs, using an oral based approach involving role play, conversation, action songs, games and rhymes. Flashcards used along with an activity book and a CD. Parents drop off child and pick up at end of session. Classes payable in advance for a term of 10–11 weeks, sessions last 30 minutes. Maximum 12 children per class. **P**

Phonics for Four Year Olds

318 Guildford Road
Bisley
Surrey GU24 9AD
01483 487714
jackie.phonics@btopenworld.com

■ *Mon–Thu and Sat am*

■ *Cost varies depending on age and length of class*

Fun learning of letter sounds and reading skills for pre-school children from $3^1/_2$ yrs, plus extra help with literacy skills from Reception to year 2. Pre-school classes last $1^1/_4$ hours, maximum of 8 children per class. Waiting list may apply. **P**

POSTNATAL EXERCISE FOR MUM

Arena Leisure Centre

01276 28787

■ *Tue 09:45–10:30*

■ *£3.65 per class*

Aqua Postnatal exercise classes offer gentle exercise both before and after baby's birth. Instructor qualified to teach post natal classes, babies can attend the class. Crèche available during classes. (See main entry for full details of amenities)

Dolphin Yoga

The Vyne Centre
45 Broadway
Knaphill
Woking
Surrey GU21 2SP
Jan Nunney 01483 740116
www.dolphinyoga.co.uk
jan@dolphinyoga.co.uk

■ *£20 per course*

Postnatal yoga course of 4 weeks, babies welcome at class. Also regular schedule of gentle yoga, also suitable for postnatal mums. **P**

Dunk your Bump - Guildford Spectrum

01483 443322

■ *Tue 11:00–12:00 and Wed 20:00–21:00*

■ *£3.90 per class*

A gentle aqua exercise class for both before and after baby's birth taken by midwives from the Royal Surrey County Hospital, babies can attend the class. See main entry under Sports and Leisure Centres for full details of amenities.

Post/ and Antenatal Exerciser – Guildford Spectrum

01483 443322

■ *Mon 11:00–12:00 and Thu 11:05–12:05*

■ *£3.30 per class*

Easy to follow exercise class for women who want to maintain fitness before and after baby's birth. Classes are taken by trained midwives, qualified in post/ante natal exercise, babies can attend the class. See main entry under Sports and Leisure Centres for full details of amenities.

Postnatal Aqua Exercise – Pool in the Park

01483 771122

■ *Fri 13:30–14:30*

■ *£3.90 per class*

Aqua Postnatal exercise classes offer gentle exercise after baby's birth. Instructor qualified to teach post natal classes, babies can attend the class. Antenatal also available. Crèche not available during Postnatal class. See main entry under Sports and Leisure

Centres for full details of amenities.

Postnatal Yoga

Swami Satvikananda 01932 872587

■ *Mon 18:30–20:00 Virginia Water Community Centre*

■ *£7 per class or £35 for set of 6 classes*

Yoga class for before and after baby's birth, qualified teacher, babies can attend the class.

Willow Sanctuary Yoga

Michelle Morrow 01483 824838

Mich_Morrow@hotmail.com

■ *Days and times by arrangement*

■ *£9 per class, usually booked in blocks of 5 or 10 weeks*

Yoga class for before and after baby's birth, qualified teacher, babies can attend the class.

SPORTS AND LEISURE CENTRES AND SWIMMING POOLS

Arena Leisure Centre

Grand Avenue
Camberley
Surrey GU15 3QH
01276 28787

www.arenaleisurecentre.co.uk
enquiries@arenaleisurecentre.co.uk

■ *Mon–Sun*

■ *Cost varies according to facilities used and time of day- contact centre for details*

Leisure centre with full range of amenities for both adults and children. Various clubs including badminton, trampolining, ballet, martial arts and the Fun House club for children, Crazy Creepers for 0–5yrs, Crazy Gang for 5–7yrs. Crazy Creepers offer a range of activities throughout the week which include arts and craft sessions, music and movement classes, trampolining, bouncy castle and soft play. Two indoor pools, main pool and teaching pool for under 8yrs – Bobbing Babes session exclusively for under 3's. Café bar for refreshments and organised birthday parties service offered.

Coral Reef – Bracknell's Waterworld

Nine Mile Ride
Bracknell
Berkshire
RG12 7JQ
01344 862525

www.bracknell-forest.gov.uk/coralreef
coral.reef@bracknell-forest.gov.uk

■ *Mon–Sun*

■ *Cost varies according to facilities used and time of day – contact centre for details*

Indoor and outdoor pool complex with various features including Little Corals toddlers pool, Pirate Ship with water cannons, Blue Lagoon Bubble Lounger, Wild Water Rapids and Snake River Flumes. Centre offers pre-school swimming lessons, parent and toddler sessions and birthday parties. Bar and restaurant for refreshments.

Guildford Spectrum

Parkway
Guildford
Surrey GU1 1UP
01483 443322

www.guildfordspectrum.co.uk
info@guildfordspectrum.co.uk

■ *Mon–Sun*

■ *Cost varies according to facilities used and time of day – contact centre for*

details
Leisure complex with large selection of amenities and activities for adults and children, including ice skating, tenpin bowling and martial arts. Pool complex includes Leisure pool with flume rides, wave machine and Toddler Splash sessions, Teaching pool, Competition pool and Diving pool, plus a wide range of spectator events including ice shows and music concerts. Softplay area for toddlers, Cosmic Kids club offers savings on combinations of activities for 4–10yr olds. Cafés and bars for refreshments.

Guildford Lido

Stoke Road
Guildford
Surrey GU1 1HB
01483 444888
www.guildford.gov.uk/guildfordweb/leisure/guildford+lido
lido@guildford.gov.uk

■ *May-Sept: Mon–Sun 10:30-18:30*
■ *Cost £4 for adults and £3 for under 16yrs*
Outdoor swimming pool set in land-scaped gardens the Lido has a heated, 50 metre pool and restored changing facilities. The pool is also available for clubs and private hire. Access for wheelchairs is limited. P

Woking Pool in the Park

Woking Park
Kingfield Road
Woking
Surrey GU22 9BA
01483 771122
www.woking.gov.uk/leisure/recreation/venues/pool

■ *Mon–Sun*
■ *Cost varies according to facilities used and time of day – contact centre for details*
Indoor pool complex which includes Competition Pool with graded lanes, Leisure Lagoon with wave machine, waterfalls and fountains, river rapids ride and three flumes and Teaching Pool. Centre offers comprehensive program of swimming lessons for children and adults as well as water aerobics and parent and toddler splash sessions with floats and aquatic toys in the Lagoon. Crèche in the Leisure Centre is available to parents of children aged 1-4yrs11mths.
P

Woking Leisure Centre

Woking Park
Kingfield Road
Woking
Surrey GU22 9BA
01483 771122

■ *Mon–Sun*
■ *Cost varies according to facilities used and time of day – contact centre for details*
Leisure Complex with various facilities for adults and children including Sensations multi-sensory suite, plus Pick 'n' Mix softplay, PlaySchool mornings for the under 5yrs and Jambulaka musical playtime sessions. Birthday party service offered. The Games Hut in Woking Park is open from May to Sep each year for the public to enjoy tennis and golf activities, bowls (woods can be hired), crazy golf and putting (9 or 18 holes). The Games Hut is staffed Mon-Sun 10:00-20:00, including Bank Holidays. When a staff member is not available, then equipment can be obtained from the Leisure Centre reception. Crèche open mornings only during term-time.
P

Places to go

THIS SECTION includes a wide range of places to go and has been divided into four sections. We have organised the attractions into those that are mainly indoors and those that are mainly outdoors to give you somewhere to go whatever the weather!

We have included attractions that are outside Surrey but are generally within an hour's drive of Woking. We felt that many of them had something special to offer and so are worth the extra travel time.

The playground section includes postcodes for the nearest road, to help you locate them as some can be difficult to find. Woking is currently undergoing a considerable amount of development and new playgrounds continue to appear all the time, consequently our list cannot be complete but it is comprehensive.

For very young children a walk in the woods or a visit to the park is every bit as exciting as some of the more sophisticated, and more expensive attractions we've listed, hence our inclusion of the walks and woodlands section. It lists many places where you can go for a quiet stroll and let your little ones let off some steam, without being out of pocket.

We've done our best to provide accurate information, but pricing and times may be subject to change, so you should always phone or check the internet before setting out on your trip.

We hope this section helps you keep your children entertained and you sane !

ATTRACTIONS INDOORS

Airborne Forces Museum

Browning Barracks
Aldershot
Hampshire GU11 2BU
01252 349619
www.parachuteregiment.com/museum

■ *Daily 10:00–16:00*
■ *Adult £2.50, child £1.50, other concessions available*

Traces the history of British airborne forces since the beginning in 1940 to the present day. P

Baron's Cave & Tunnel Road Caves

Castle Grounds
Reigate
Surrey RH2 9AT
01306 742551
www.wcms.org.uk
info@wcms.org.uk

■ *various Sat during Summer*

Private tours and visits may be arranged for small groups. The cave is one of Britain's oldest show caves. It is part of the old Norman castle, which was demolished many years ago. Entrance close to Boots on the High Street. Access is via a short flight of steps. P

Blue Reef Aquarium

Clarence Esplanade
Southsea
Portsmouth
Hampshire PO5 3PB
023 9287 5222
www.bluereefaquarium.co.uk

■ *Daily except Christmas Day from 10:00. Closing times vary throughout the year*
■ *Adult £5.95, child £3.95, under 3yrs free.*
■ *M27 to Portsmouth, then follow signs to Southsea and brown tourist signs*

Ultimate undersea safari ranging from life in British waters to tropical coral reefs. Shop. Café with highchairs and children's menu. Parking on esplanade or large car park next door. Birthday parties catered for, also special events and workshops. P

Brooklands Motor and Aviation Museum

Brooklands Road
Weybridge
Surrey KT13 0QN
01932 857381
www.brooklandsmuseum.com

■ *Winter: Tue-Sun and Bank Holidays 10:00–16:00*
Summer: Tue-Sun and Bank Holidays 10:00–17:00
■ *Adults £7.00, child £5.00, under 6yrs free plus family tickets and other concessions available*
■ *A245 through West Byfleet and on to Byfleet. The museum is off the B374 towards Weybridge; follow the brown signs.*

Museum for historic cars and aeroplanes located on 30 acres of the 1907 motor-racing circuit. Many original buildings restored, period room settings, over 30 aircraft. Access to aircraft. Diary of special events organised throughout the year (phone for details). Grassy areas for children to run around. Gift shop. Restaurant/tea room with children's menu and highchairs. Public car park and some spaces at front of building. P

Cobham Bus Museum

The London Bus Prevention Trust
Redhill Road
Cobham
Surrey KT11 1EF
01932 868665

■ *Wed, Sat-Sun 10:00–17:00 but children recommended to attend theme days which take place once a month (phone for details)*
■ *Free entry but for themed days adult £4.00, in April adult £7.00, under 16 yrs free if accompanied by an adult*
■ *Follow A245 through Byfleet, turn right into Redhill Road, museum is immediately on left.*
A collection of circa 30 ex-London transport vehicles from 1925 – 1979. Wheelchair and buggy access limited except on theme days when provision is made and vehicles on display are open for entry and rides. Café. **P**

Guildford Cathedral
Stag Hill
Guildford GU2 7UP
01483 565287
01483 547860 (Group Booking)
01483 725432 (Brass Rubbing Parties)
www.guildford-cathedral.org

■ *Brass Rubbing Centre Apr-Oct: Mon-Sat 10:00–12:00 and 14:00–16:00 for casual visitors. All year round for parties and pre-booked groups.*
■ *Free entry*
■ *From A3, come off at Park Barn/ university exit. Cathedral is on left.*
Modern cathedral and brass rubbing centre. Refectory open daily 09:30-16:00 and has 1 highchair. **P**

Heathrow Airport Visitor Centre
Newall Road
Heathrow Airport
Hounslow
Middlesex UB3 5AP
020 8745 6655
www.baa.co.uk

■ *Daily except Christmas Day and Boxing Day 10:00–17:00*
■ *Free entry. Pay and Display car park in front of centre with special parking for disabled access*
■ *Off the A4 Bath Road close to the Renaissance Hotel via the Airport's northern perimeter road.*
Colourful, interactive exhibits displaying the story of Heathrow's past, present and future as well as information on airport policy and operations. Cockpit simulator. Coffee shop with light refreshments. Outside picnic area with tables and benches.

The Living Rainforest
Hampstead Norreys
Thatcham
Berkshire RG18 0TN
01635 202444
www.livingrainforest.org

■ *Daily except Christmas Day and Boxing Day 10:00–17:15*
■ *Adults £4.95, children 5-14 yrs £3.25, children 3-4yrs £1.95, under 3yrs free, family tickets plus other concessions available*
■ *J13 of M4 – estimated just over 1 hour drive.*
A tropical rainforest and inspired ecological garden. Exotic plants and wildlife including giant Amazon water lilies, a rare Jade vine and monkeys. Some minor restrictions to double buggy and wheelchair access due to plant growth. Café. Can also picnic in gardens. Educational talks, varied events and children's birthday parties catered for. **P**

National Motor Museum and John Montagu Building
Beaulieu
Brockenhurst
Hampshire SO42 7ZN
01590 612345
www.beaulieu.co.uk

■ *May-Sep: daily except Christmas Day*

10:00–18:00, Oct-Mar: 10:00-17:00
■ *Adult £13.50, child £6.50, under 5yrs free and family tickets and other concessions available*
■ *Take M3, then M27 westwards, then A326 and follow the brown tourist signs.*
Motor car collection. Palace House and gardens, 13th Century abbey and rides. Extensive grounds, high level monorail, replica 1912 open-topped bus, mini-bikes and miniature veteran cars, over 250 vehicles–some dating from the 1890's. Shop. Restaurant and café with children's menu and highchairs.

Shere Museum

The Malt House
Shere Lane
Shere
Surrey GU5 9HS
01483 203245

■ *Easter-end Sep: Mon-Tue, Thu-Fri and Sun 13:00–17:00.*
Other times by arrangement
■ *Adult £0.50, child £0.25, under 5yrs free*
■ *From A25 to Dorking, turn right into Rectory Lane in Shere. Follow road round in to Lower Street and turn right into Shere Lane.*
Village museum containing various artefacts from local area including old toys and books. Games, puzzles and quiz sheets available and a toy box for small children; also sometimes a magic lantern show. Public toilets in village (200 yards). Public parking in the village, disabled parking by arrangement. Small gift shop and refreshments available for groups by arrangement.

OUTDOOR ATTRACTIONS

Alice Holt Woodland Park Centre

Bucks Horn Oak
Farnham
Surrey GU10 4LS
01420 23666
www.forestry.gov.uk

■ *Daily dawn to dusk*
■ *Free to use Park but £2 charge for parking*
■ *Off A325 to Portsmouth just past Birdworld.*
Woodland park and working forest. Visitor Centre, play areas, marked walks, cycle paths, picnic areas, shop selling snacks and drinks. Cycles available for hire weekends and holidays including trailers for small children. Programme of activities organised in holidays. Leaflet available showing walks suitable for wheelchairs and pushchairs.

Basingstoke Canal Visitor Centre

Mychett Place Road
Mytchett
Surrey GU16 6DD
01252 370073
www.basingstoke-canal.org.uk

■ *Easter-Sep: Tue-Fri 10:30-17:30, Sat-Sun and Bank Holidays 11:00-17:30, Oct to Easter: Tue-Fri 11:00-16:00*
■ *Free entry*
■ *Mytchett Place Road off A321 in Mytchett.*
Information centre to help you get out and enjoy the canal. Small history exhibition. Fishing permits and boat licences on sale. Boat trips, day boat hire and caravan and camping site. Regular events and attractions. Restaurant serving cooked meals and snacks, and providing 2 course Sunday lunch that needs to be pre-booked (07899 701041).

Beale Park

The Child-Beale Trust
Lower Basildon
Reading
Berkshire RG8 9NH
0118 984 5172
www.bealepark.co.uk
bealepark@bun.com

■ *1st Mar-31st Oct: daily 10:00-18:00 Winter: daily 10:00-17:00 or dusk, whichever is earlier*
■ *Adults £5.50, children 3-16yrs £4.00, under 3yrs free, further concessions available*
■ *6 miles south of Reading on A329 Reading to Oxford Road.*

Tranquil nature park beside the River Thames. Includes duck ponds, aviaries, owleries, pets corner and animal handling, deer park, piggery, flamingos, miniature goats, wallabies, steam engine, sandpits, paddling pools, adventure playground, mini funfair and picnic areas. Also narrow gauge railway and river cruises at an extra charge. All areas accessible by pushchair. Café with children's menu and highchairs available. Will microwave baby food and milk on request. New toddlers play area and giant aviaries under construction.

Bekonscot Model Village

Warwick Road
Beaconsfield
Buckinghamshire HP9 2PL
01494 672919
www.bekonscot.com

■ *Feb-Oct: daily 10:00-17:00*
■ *Adults £4.80, children £3, children under 3yrs free, family ticket and further concessions available*
■ *Signposted from Junction 2 of the M40.*

Oldest model village in world. Includes an airport, coal mine, funfair and railway. Also has ride on train at extra charge. All areas accessible by pushchair but double buggy may be tight in some places. Picnic area and café serving hot and cold food with highchairs available. Will warm baby food and milk on request. Gift shop. Birthday parties catered for.

Birdworld and Underwater World

Holt Pound
Farnham
Surrey GU10 4LD
01420 22140 (Enquiries)
01420 22838 (Recorded Information)
01420 22992 (Bookings)
www.birdworld.co.uk

■ *Summer: 10:00-18:00 Winter: 10:00-16:30*
■ *Adults £9.75, children £6.95, under 3yrs free, family tickets available*
■ *From A31 Guildford to Alton Road, take A325 through Wrecclesham. Well signposted.*

Large collection of birds including Penguin Island, seashore and tropical walks. Farm and tropical aquarium. Heron Theatre where birds perform tricks and safari rides on train through park. All areas accessible by pushchair. May be difficult to get double buggy into Underwater World. Restaurant serving hot and cold food, snack kiosks and picnic areas. Will warm baby food and milk on request. Birthday parties catered for, Santa at Christmas and activity weekends.

Bluebell Railway

Sheffield Park Station
Uckfield
East Sussex TN22 3QL
01825 722370 (Information Line)
01825 720800 (Group Bookings and Additional Information)
www.bluebell-railway.co.uk

■ *11:00-16:00 for museum, shop and loco sheds, check timetable for trains*

■ *Adult £8.50, child £4.20, under 3yrs free, family tickets and further concessions available*
■ *On A275 East Grinstead to Lewes Road, 2 miles north of junction with A272.*
UK's first preserved standard gauge passenger railway. Stepney club for up to age 8 includes discounted train travel and other attractions. Access onto trains for wheelchairs via double door. Need to ring first to check if in operation. Picnic areas. Restaurant at Sheffield Park and other facilities at other stations.

Bocketts Farm Park

Young Street
Fetcham
Surrey KT22 9BS
01372 363764
www.bockettsfarm.co.uk
■ *Summer: 10:00-18:00*
Winter: 10:00-dusk
■ *Adults £4.35, children 3-17yrs £3.95, 3yrs £3.25, under 2yrs free, further concessions available*
■ *Off the A426 Guildford to Epsom Road, near Leatherhead.*
Working farm with play barn and extensive play area. Ride on toys, sandpit, climbing frames, trampolines and animal handling sessions. Pony rides and tractor rides at extra charge. All areas accessible by pushchair though some areas can be muddy. Tea barn, outdoor seating area and picnic areas. Will warm baby food and milk on request. Birthday parties catered for. Santa's grotto at Christmas.

British Wildlife Centre

Newchapel
Lingfield
Surrey RH7 6LF
01342 834658
www.britishwildlifecentre.co.uk
info@britishwildlifecentre.co.uk
■ *Easter-end Oct: all school holidays, Sundays and Bank Holidays 10:00-17:00*
■ *Adult £6.50, child 3-14yrs £5, under 3yrs free, family tickets available*
■ *On A22 between Blindley Heath and Newchapel.*
Large enclosures with 300 species of wildlife, badgers sett, museum, Visitor Centre, lecture theatre and picnic areas. All areas accessible by pushchair. Café serving sandwiches and cakes with highchairs available. Parties catered for.

Bucklebury Farm Park

Bucklebury
Reading
Berkshire RG7 6RR
01189 971 4002
www.buckleburyfarmpark.co.uk
■ *22nd Mar-21st Sep: daily 10:00-18:00*
27th Sep-26th Oct: Sat-Sun only, daily during Autumn half term
■ *Adult £4.25, child £3, under 3yrs free, further concessions available*
■ *On edge of Bucklebury village, 3.5 miles from A4 between Reading and Newbury.*
Farm park with farm animals, red deer herd, rabbits, adventure playground and 2 mile walk. All areas accessible by pushchair. Snacks and drinks available. Birthday parties catered for.

Burpham Court Farm

Clay Lane
Jacobs Well
Surrey GU4 7NA
01483 576089
www.burphamcourtfarm.org
■ *Summer: 10:00-18:00*
Winter: 10:00-18:00 or dusk
■ *Adult £3.95, child £2.95, under 2yrs free, further concessions available*
■ *Head towards Guildford on A320, turn*

left into Clay Lane at Jacob's Well. Follow brown tourist signs.

Small working farm with rare breed's collection, conservation centre and Nature Trail. Egg collecting and animal handling possible. Most areas accessible by pushchair but ground may be muddy and uneven. Café with highchair available. No baby change area but changing mat available on request. Will warm baby food and milk on request. Small play area with swings, tractor, sandpit. Birthday parties catered for.

Chessington World of Adventures

Chessington
Surrey KT9 2NE
0870 444 7777
www.chessington.co.uk

■ *End Mar-Sep: 10:00-18:00*
■ *Adult £24, child age 4-11yrs £18, under 4yrs free, further concessions available*
■ *On A243 Leatherhead Road.*

Large theme park with rides and zoo including activities for little ones such as Toy Town. All areas accessible by pushchair. Lots of cafés and restaurants situated throughout park. Baby food and milk can be warmed at the medical centre.

Cholderton Rare Breeds Farm Park and Rabbit World

Amesbury Road
Cholderton
Salisbury
Wiltshire SP4 0EW
01980 629438
www.rabbitworld.co.uk

■ *Mid Mar-beg Nov: Mon-Sun 10:00-18:00 Winter: Sat-Sun 10:00-16:00*
■ *Adult £5.50, child 2-16yrs £3.50, under 2yrs free, further concessions available*
■ *Off A303/A338, west of Andover.*

Small farm park with farm animals. Pets corner, animal walking, pony rides, small play areas, mini Go-Karts, trampoline and picnic areas. Tractor and trailer rides at additional cost. Tea room with children's menu, highchairs and play area. Will microwave baby food and milk on request. All areas accessible by pushchair but hard going on grass.

Clandon Park (National Trust)

West Clandon
Guildford
Surrey GU4 7RQ
01483 222482
01483 225971 (Infoline)
www.nationaltrust.org.uk

■ *28th Mar–31st Oct: Tue-Thu and Sun 11:00–17:00*
■ *Adults £6, child £3, family tickets available*
■ *At West Clandon on A247, 3 miles east of Guildford; if using A3 follow signposts to Ripley to join A247 via B2215*

Grand 18th-century Palladian mansion, Clandon is notable for its magnificent two-storeyed Marble Hall and filled with a superb collection of 18th-century furniture, porcelain, textiles and carpets. The gardens contain a parterre, grotto, sunken Dutch garden and a Maori meeting house with a fascinating history. Licensed restaurant with children's menu. Front-carrying baby slings and hip-carrying infant seats for loan. Children's quiz/trail. Pushchairs allowed in house Tue-Thu.

Dapdune Wharf

National Trust
Wharf Road
Guildford
Surrey GU1 4RR
01483 561389

www.nationaltrust.org.uk
■ *Mar-Nov: Thu-Mon 11:00-17:00*
■ *Adult £3.00, child 5-17yrs £1.50, towpath free, further concessions available*
■ *From Guildford town centre, take Woodbridge Road towards Ladymead. Turn left into Wharf Road just before cricket ground.*
Visitor Centre describing history of the River Wey and Navigation. Interactive displays, moored barge to visit and boat trips available. Boat trips available on horse drawn barges, row boats, canoes, narrow boats, restaurant boats and excursion boats. $19^{1}/_{2}$ mile towpath open to walkers. Café. Access is with care.

Denbies Wine Estate

London Road
Dorking
Surrey RH5 6AA
01306 876616
www.denbiesvineyard.co.uk
info@denbiesvineyard.co.uk
■ *Winery tours and tasting: Jan-Mar: Mon-Fri on the hour 11:00-15:00 (no 13:00 tour), Sat 11:00-16:00 (no 13:00 tour), Sun 12:00-16:00*
Apr-Dec: Mon –Sat on the hour 11:00-16:00 (no 13:00 tour), Sun 12:00-16:00
Vineyard train tour (ring for confirmation): Apr-Sep: Mon-Sun on the hour 11:00-16:00 (no 13:00 tour)
Oct : Mon-Sun on the hour 11:00-15:00 (no 13:00 tour)
■ *Vineyard train tour: adults £4.00, child 6-16yrs £3.00, under 5 yrs free. Winery tour and tasting: adults £7.25, child 6-17yrs £3.00, under 5 yrs free*
■ *On A24 on outskirts of Dorking.*
Indoor winery tour including 'people-mover' train and wine tasting (grape juice for children). Outdoor vineyard train tour up into the hills. All areas accessible by pushchair but no push-chairs on train. Restaurant which also provides children's lunchboxes and has bead maze. Highchairs available and will warm baby food and milk on request.

Drusillas Park

Alfriston
East Sussex BN26 5QS
01323 874100
www.drusillas.co.uk
drusilla@drusilla.demon.co.uk
■ *Summer: daily 10:00-17:00*
Winter: daily (except Christmas Eve, Christmas Day and Boxing Day) 10:00-16:00
■ *Adult £9.49, child 3-12yrs £8.49, under 2yrs free*
■ *Off A27 Eastbourne to Brighton Road, north of Alfriston.*
Zoo, petting barn, free train rides, large children's play area, trampolines, children's paddling pool, picnic areas. Adventure golf and Wacky Workshop at extra charge. All areas accessible by pushchair. Restaurant with children's menu, baby food and highchairs. Indoor children's play area in restaurant. Café serving fast food. Will warm baby food and milk on request. Birthday parties catered for.

Farnham Castle Keep

Castle Hill
Farnham
Surrey GU9 0AE
01252 713393 (Recorded Message)
www.english-heritage.org.uk
■ *Apr-Sep: Sat-Sun 10:00-17:00*
■ *Adults £2.50, Children £1.30, other concessions available*
■ *A287 north of Farnham town centre*
This motte-and-bailey castle has been continuously occupied since the 12th century and was once one of the seats of the Bishop of Winchester. Audio tours available. Shop. Good access to castle,

but access to keep is via uneven steps, therefore unsuitable for wheelchairs.

P

Finkley Down Farm Park

Andover
Hampshire SP11 6NF
01264 324141
01264 352195 (24 hour information line)
www.finkleydownfarm.co.uk

■ *Mid Mar-end Oct: daily 10:00-18:00*
■ *Adult £5, child 2-14yrs £4, under 2yrs free and other concessions available*
■ *North of the A303, 2 miles east of Andover.*

Shire horses, mini tractors, farm animals, aviary, toddler playground, playground, trampolines, sandpit, picnic areas and undercover areas. All areas accessible by pushchair. Tea room which will warm baby food and milk on request. Birthday parties catered for.

P

Fishers Farm Park

Newpound Lane
Wisborough Green
West Sussex RH14 0EG
01403 700603
www.fishersfarmpark.co.uk
info@fishersfarmpark.co.uk

■ *Daily 10:00-17:00*
■ *Adult £6.25-£8.25, child 3-16yrs £5.75-£7.75, 2yrs £2.50-4.50, under 2yrs free, further concessions available, seasonal variation in charges*
■ *Off B2133 past Loxwood via the A281 from Guildford.*

Farm with range of farm and pet animals. Outdoor adventure play areas, bumper boats, climbing wall, trampolines, bouncy castles, giant paddling pool, giant sandpit, indoor soft play area. Theatre with magic, farm show, clown, vet talks. Café serving hot food and snacks with highchairs available. Birthday parties catered for.

P

French Brothers Ltd

The Clewer Boathouse
Clewer Court Road
Windsor
Berkshire SL4 5JH
01753 851900
www.boat-trips.org.uk

■ *Easter-Sep: daily from 11:00*
■ *Adult from £4.40, child from £2.20*
■ *Off A308 in Windsor.*

Boat trips on the River Thames from Windsor or Runnymede. All areas accessible by pushchair but not much space on board. No café on board but facilities at Runnymede Pleasure Gardens and Magna Carta Tea Rooms in Windsor. No toilets on board but facilities at Runnymede Pleasure Gardens. Parking is in pay and display public car parks.

Frimley Lodge Park

Sturt Road
Frimley Green
Surrey GU16 6HY
01252 836970
www.blackwater-valley.org.uk

■ *All year daily*
■ *Free entry*
■ *Off A321 towards Mytchett.*

59 acres of grass meadows, hedgerows, habitat for flora and fauna situated adjacent to the Basingstoke canal. Two play areas, pitch and putt, woodland and canal side walks, trim trail, picnic and barbecue areas. Home to Frimley Lodge Miniature Railway Society. All areas accessible by pushchair. Café.

P

Gatton Park Education Trust

Gatton Park
Reigate
Surrey RH2 0TD
01737 649066
www.gatton-park.org.uk
education@gatton-park.org.uk

■ *Feb-Oct: first Sunday of month 13:00-17:00*
■ *Adult £2, children free*
■ *Can be reached from A23 past Merstham or A242 from Reigate.*
Historic parkland with woodland trails, historic buildings, special toddler trail, lake and holiday activities. Accessible by pushchair except for parts of Gatton Hall. Tea and cakes in Gatton Hall.

Godalming Packetboat Company

57 Furze Lane
Farncombe
Godalming
Surrey GU7 3NP
01483 414938
www.horseboat.org.uk

■ *Easter-end Sep: most days starting at 14:30*
■ *Adult or child £5.00*
■ *A3100 Guildford to Godalming Road, turn left from Bridge Road into Flambard Way and then left again into Woolsack Way.*
Narrow boat pulled by heavy horse along river and canal passing through a lock. Tea bar on board. Access for pushchairs and wheelchairs may be difficult. Parking is on road or in Godalming with walk to river.

Godstone Farm

Tilburstow Hill Road
Godstone
Surrey RH9 8LX
01883 742546
www.godstonefarm.co.uk
havefun@godstonefarm.co.uk

■ *Summer: daily 10:00-18:00*
Winter: daily 10:00-17:00
■ *Adult £4.80, under 2yrs free*
■ *From M25 Junction 6 follow signs through village of Godstone.*
Working farm with many young animals, nature trail, picnic area, sandpit and adventure playground for older children. Undercover barns with ride on toys, spinning room, bee room and lambing. All areas accessible by pushchair. Café with children's menu and highchairs. Will warm baby food and milk on request. Birthday parties catered for.

Great Cockcrow Miniature Railway

Hardwick Lane
Lyne
Chertsey
Surrey KT16 0AD
01932 565474 (Sun only)
01932 255500 (Mon–Fri for bookings onto Gladesman)
www.guess99.freeserve.co.uk/gcrtrain.htm

■ *Easter-end Oct: Sun 14:00-17:30*
■ *Adult £2.50, Children over 2yrs £2, other fares apply*
■ *A320 to St Peter's Hospital, at roundabout take B386 left (Holloway Hill) and right onto Hardwick Lane.*
Steam and diesel locomotives run at various times around this mile long track, with journeys lasting about 20 minutes. Gladesman only runs at 17:00 and the journey lasts 25 minutes but can be booked in advance. Parties and other bookings by arrangement. Kiosk selling refreshments and picnic area.

Guildford Boathouse Ltd

Millbrook
Guildford
Surrey GU1 3JX
01483 536186 (Talking Timetable)
01483 504494
www.guildfordboats.co.uk

■ *Easter-Jul: Wed, Sat-Sun and Bank Holidays*
Jul-Sep: Tue-Thu, Sat-Sun and Bank Holidays

■ *Adult from £3.00, child from £1.75, under 5yrs free*
■ *From Guildford town centre, take A281 Horsham Road. Fork left for Millbrook car park. Take first right into Quarry Street. Turn right at traffic lights and left into car park.*
Public trips on a riverboat between Guildford and Godalming. Quayside accessible for pushchair, double buggy and wheelchair. Kiosk selling hot and cold drinks. Parking in Millbrook pay and display.

Hampton Court

Hampton Court Palace
East Molesey
Surrey KT8 9AU
0870 752 7777
www.hrp.org.uk/webcode/hampton_home.asp

■ *Adult £11.80, children 5-16yrs £7.70, under 5yrs free*
■ *House open Mar-Oct: Mon 10:15-18:00, Tue-Sun 09:30-18:00*
Oct-Mar: Mon 10:15-16:30, Tue-Sun 09:30-16:30 (closed 24-26 Dec inc)
Gardens open: all year 07:00-dusk
■ *M25 exit 10 on to the A307 or exit 12 on to the A308. From the A3 take the A309 turning*
This royal palace contains magnificent state apartments, costumed guides, works of art, 60 acres of riverside gardens and 500 years of royal history. There is a designated Family Room where parents and young children can rest and use the play equipment which is all suitable for children under 5yrs. Family Trails which guide children around the palace are available. Access is good but pathways are cobbled. A pushchair park is available and lifts to upper floors. Fees for parking apply.

Hatchlands Park (National Trust)

East Clandon
Guildford
GU4 7RT
01483 222482
01483 225971 (Information Line)
www.nationaltrust.org.uk
hatchlands@nationaltrust.org.uk

■ *House open Apr-Jul: Tue-Thu and Sun 14:00-17:30*
Aug: Tue-Fri 14:00-17:30
Sep-Oct: Tue-Thu and Sun 14:00-17:30
Park walks open Mar-Oct: 11:00-18:00
■ *Adult £6, children £3, other concessions available. Park walks only: £2.50, child £1.25*
■ *North of A246 Guildford to Leatherhead road*
Stately home with Cobbe collection of keyboard instruments, paintings and furniture. Extensive grounds with a small formal garden, an icehouse, temple, bluebell woods, park walks, shop and tearoom. Wheelchair access to ground floor of house. Front carrying baby slings and hip carrying infant seats available to hire. Children's quiz trail available. P

Hawk Conservancy

Wey Hill
Andover
Hampshire SP11 8DY
01264 772252
www.hawk-conservancy.org
info@hawk-conservancy.org

■ *First Sat of Spring half term-last Sat in Autumn half term: daily 10:30-17:30*
■ *Adult £6.95, child £4.35, further concessions available*
■ *Signposted from A303, west of Andover.*
Conservancy with flying displays, bird feeding, nature trail, ferret racing, duck racing, education centre, picnic area, children's adventure play areas and tiny

toddlers enclosed play area. All areas accessible by pushchair and has won a Disability Access award. Coffee shop with children's menu including lunch box. Will microwave baby food and milk on request. Birthday parties can be for. 'Owls by torchlight' and activity days sometimes arranged.

Hollycombe Steam Fairground

Iron Hill
Liphook
Hampshire GU30 7LP
01428 724900
www.hollycombe.co.uk

■ *Apr-beg Oct: Sun and Bank Holidays Aug: daily 12:00–17:00*
■ *Adult £8.50, Children £7, concessions and family tickets available*
■ *2 miles off A3 at Liphook*

Britain's largest steam fairground with steam railways, traction engine hauled rides, farm area, woodland gardens and picnic areas. Some rides suitable for wheelchair users.

Holmbush Farm World

Faygate
Horsham
West Sussex RH12 4SE
01293 851110
www.holmbushfarm.co.uk

■ *Mid Mar-end Oct: daily 10:00-17:30*
■ *Adult £4.00, child £3.50, further concessions available*
■ *Off A264.*

Working farm with range of farm and pet animals. Tractor rides, play areas including sand pits and tree houses. All areas accessible by pushchair. Tea room serving hot and cold meals. Will warm baby food and milk on request. Children's parties catered for.

Horton Park Children's Farm

Horton Lane
Epsom
Surrey KT19 8PT
01372 743984
www.hortonpark.co.uk
childrensfarm@hortonpark.co.uk

■ *Summer: daily 10:00-18:00*
Winter: daily 10:00-17:00
■ *Adult and one child £4.30, under 2yrs free*
■ *From M25 Junction 9, take A243 to Chessington, turn right onto B280 to Epsom, at first roundabout turn left then follow signs.*

Farm park where children are able to handle and touch the animals. Ride on tractors, indoor soft play area and outdoor play area with sandpit, straw pit, castle, scramble nets and more. Separate enclosed toddler area. All areas accessible by pushchair. Tea room serving hot and cold food. Picnic areas. Will warm baby food and milk on request. Birthday parties catered for.

Hounslow Urban Farm

Faggs Road
Feltham
Middlesex TW14 0LZ
020 8751 0850
www.cip.com
urbanfarm@cip.org.uk

■ *Feb-Oct: Tue-Sun 10:00-16:00 (open Bank Holiday Mondays)*
Summer holidays: 10:00-17:00
■ *Adult £3.00, child £1.50, under 2yrs free, further concessions available*
■ *Can be reached from A312 or A30 at Hatton Cross.*

Working farm with range of domesticated animals, play area, ride on tractors. All areas accessible by pushchair. Café.

John Pinkerton Canal Boat Trip

Departures from Ash Wharf Bridge,
Fox and Hounds pub Fleet,
Colt Hill Odiham
01962 713564 (Booking Line)
www.basingstokecanal1.freeserve.co.uk/jpink.htm

■ *1st May-Oct: Third Sun of the month at 14:30*
■ *Adult £5, child £2*
■ *Both Odiham and Dogmersfield are reached from A287 from Farnham.*

Two and a half hour round trip on the Basingstoke canal. Pushchairs need to be lifted down 4 steps. Although pushchairs, double buggies and wheelchairs are welcome on the boat, no person must be moved by volunteers, crew or helpers. Bar serving light refreshments. Will warm baby food and milk on request. There is room to play on the boat but best to make prior arrangements. Children must be supervised at all times.

Legoland

Winkfield Road
Windsor
Berkshire SL4 4AY
08705 040404 (Information)
01753 626111
www.legoland.co.uk

■ *Mar-Nov: daily 10:00-17:00 (closing time varies with season)*
■ *Adult £22.95, child £19.95, under 3yrs free, further concessions available, off-peak rates cheaper*
■ *From A322 to Bracknell, take A332, then B3022 Windsor/Ascot Road.*

The park is set within 150 acres of landscaped gardens with a range of activities to suit all ages with rides, water splashes, trains, large scale Lego models, hands on play with Lego. All areas accessible by pushchair. Can hire pushchairs, wheelchairs and kennels. 10 different restaurants all with different themes plus covered and uncovered picnic areas. Highchairs and booster seats available. Will warm baby food and milk on request in care centre.

Lockwood Donkey Sanctuary

Farm Cottage
Hatch Lane
Sandhills
Wormey
Godalming
Surrey GU8 5UX
01428 682409

■ *365 days a year: daily 09:00-17:00*
■ *No admission fee but donations accepted*
■ *Take A283 Petworth Road to Wormley, and then take a right signposted Sandhills. At fork turn left, Hatch Lane is on left.*

Rescue animal centre with donkeys, pigs, llamas, rabbits and goats. Carrots available to feed animals. Lots of different animals available to adopt.

The Look Out Discovery Centre

Nine Mile Ride
Bracknell
Berkshire RG12 7QW
01344 354400
01344 874611 (Mountain Bike Hire)
www.bracknell-forest.gov.uk/lookout
thelookout@bracknell-forest.gov.uk

■ *Daily except over Christmas period 10:00-17:00*
■ *All areas are free apart from exhibition: adult £4.65, child £3.10, under 4yrs free, further concessions available*
■ *Off A322 Guildford to Bracknell Road, opposite Coral Reef.*

2,600 acres of Crown Estate woodland

with walks and trails marked. Picnic area, mountain bike hire and cycle routes, adventure playground with separate areas for older and younger children and hands on science and nature exhibition. Café serving meals and snacks including children's menu. Highchairs available. Birthday parties catered for, regular special exhibitions and school holiday Fun Days.

Loseley Park

Stakes Corner Road
Guildford
Surrey GU3 1HS
01483 304440
www.loseley-park.com
enquiries@loseley-park.com

■ *House Jun-end Aug: Wed-Sun and Bank Holidays 13:00-17:00 (Guided tours) Garden, gift shop and tea room beg May - end Sep: Wed-Sun and Bank Holidays 11:00-17:00. Estate closed to public Mon and Tues*

■ *House and Garden: adult £6.00, child £3.00, under 5 yrs free, Garden only: adult £3.00, child £1.50, under 5yrs free, further concessions available*

■ *A3100 Godalming Road. Turn right towards Compton. Over railway bridge turn right into Stakescorner Road, entrance to Loseley is on left but can be easily missed.*

House set amid parkland with walled garden, moat walk and lake walk. Shop, tea room, restaurant with children's menu and highchairs, and picnic area. Will warm baby food and milk on request. All areas accessible by pushchair except upstairs of house. Events such as gardening shows held in park.

Marwell Zoological Park

Colden Common
Winchester
Hampshire SO21 1JH
01962 777407
www.marwell.org.uk

■ *Summer: daily 10:00-18:00*
Winter: daily (except Christmas Day) 10:00-16:00

■ *Adult £11.00, child 3-14yrs £7.50, under 3 yrs free, further concessions available*

■ *Off B2177 between Colden and Bishop's Waltham.*

Zoo and park with over 200 species, many endangered. Free seasonal road train, miniature railway (additional charge). All areas accessible by pushchair though lots of hills. Restaurant with children's menu and highchairs. Microwave available for public use. Kiosks also situated around the park.

Nymans Garden

Handcross
Haywards Heath
West Sussex RH17 6EB
01444 400321
www.nationaltrust.org.uk
nymans@nationaltrust.org.uk

■ *Mar-Nov: House and Garden Wed-Sun and Bank Holidays 11:00-18:00*
Nov-Mar: Garden Sat-Sun and Bank Holidays 11:00-16:00

■ *Adult £6.20, child £3.10, further concessions available and Winter weekends cheaper*

■ *South of Crawley off A23.*

House, gardens, woodland walks, picnic areas and wild garden. Children's quiz and trail, family activity packs. Family Fun Days in July. Wheelchair access to ground floor of house, child back carriers admitted to house. Hip carrying infant seats available to loan. Grounds largely accessible to pushchairs. Licensed restaurant with children's menu and highchairs.

Odds Farm Park

Wooburn Common
High Wycombe
Buckinghamshire HP10 0LX
01628 520188
www.oddsfarm.co.uk
oddsfarm@oddsfarm.co.uk

■ *14th Feb-21st Jun: Mon-Sun 10:00-17:30*
22nd Jun-5th Sep: Mon-Sun 10:00-18:00
6th Sep-31st Oct: Mon-Sun 10:00-17:30
1st Nov-11th Feb: Mon-Sun 10:00-16:30
■ *Adult £6, child 2-16yrs £5, under 2yrs free plus other concessions available*
■ *A355 to Slough from M40 Junction 2*

Farm with range of animals. Outdoor play areas including log area, under 5yrs area, sand pits and diggers. Indoor play area includes ride on tractors, bale climb, ride on toys. Tea room with highchairs and table activities for children. Sell baby food and will warm food/ milk on request. Indoor and outdoor picnic areas. Parties catered for.

Painshill Park

Portsmouth Road
Cobham
Surrey KT11 1JE
01932 868113
www.painshill.co.uk
info@painshill.co.uk

■ *Mar-Oct: Tue-Sun 10:30-18:00*
Nov-Feb: Wed-Sun (except Christmas Day) 11:00-16:00 or dusk
■ *Adult £6.00, child 5-16yrs £3.50, under 5yrs free, further concessions available*
■ *Off A245 from A3.*

18th Century landscaped park. Walks through woodland and by lakes. All areas accessible by pushchair except gothic tower. Visitor Centre, shop, picnic area and café. New education centre to facilitate school events, regular special events for children, families and adults.

Polesden Lacey (National Trust)

Great Bookham
Dorking
Surrey RH5 6BD
01372 452048
01372 458203 (Information)
www.nationaltrust.org.uk/places/polesdenlacey/
polesdenlacey@nationaltrust.org.uk

1400 acre estate situated on the North Downs with some of the finest views in Surrey. The Edwardian Garden extends to 30 acres with lawns and elegant grass terraces, including a walled rose garden, summer border and winter displays.

RHS Garden Wisley

Wisley
Woking
Surrey GU23 6QB
01483 224234
www.rhs.org.uk/gardens/wisley

■ *Feb-Nov: 10:00-18:00*
Nov-Feb: 10:00-16:30
■ *Adult £6.00, child 6-16yrs £2.00, under 6yrs free*
■ *Just off A3 heading north, south of Junction 10 with M25.*

Flagship garden of the RHS consisting of 240 acres including practiced and innovative techniques, trial fields, model gardens, and beautifully planted borders. Routes signposted for wheelchairs. Wheelchairs and pushchairs available to borrow free of charge. Large café and restaurant within garden serving range of hot and cold food, coffee shop by entrance and kiosk open in Summer. Shop and garden centre. Some areas of garden have steps so not all areas accessible by pushchair.

Royal Botanic Gardens Kew

Richmond
Surrey TW19 3AB
020 8332 5655
www.rbgkew.org.uk

■ *Daily (except Christmas Eve and Christmas Day) 09:30. Closing time depends on season.*
■ *Adult £7.50, under 16yrs free, further concessions available*
■ *On A307 just south of Kew Bridge.*

300 acres of landscaped gardens containing the world's largest collection of living plants. Four acres are under glass. Have a programme of five festivals a year, each one having children's events e.g. story telling, story walks. At Christmas, garden is lit up and has a Father Christmas. All areas accessible by pushchair except some of glasshouses. Three restaurants and one café serving range of options from sandwiches to hot meals. Two shops. Pay and Display car park or parking on surrounding roads for free.

Royal Botanic Gardens Wakehurst Place

Ardingly
Haywards Heath
West Sussex RH17 6TN
01444 894066
www.rbgkew.org.uk
wakehurst@kew.org

■ *Daily (except Christmas Eve and Christmas Day) 10:00*
■ *Adult £7.00, under 16yrs free, further concessions available*
■ *M23 Junction 10, take A264 then B2028 to Turner's Hill. Gardens are south of Turner's Hill.*

180 acres of country estate including ornamental gardens, woodland, Elizabethan Mansion House, self-guided trails, home to the Millennium Seed Bank Exhibition. Most areas suitable for pushchairs but woodland area has steep slopes and steps. Free map indicates suitable paths. Licensed restaurant serving hot and cold meals. Coffee shop in new visitor centre.

Rural Life Centre

Old Kiln Museum
Reeds Road
Tilford
Farnham
Surrey GU10 2DL
01252 795571
www.rural-life.org.uk
rural.life@lineone.net

■ *Mar-Oct: Wed-Sun 10:00-17:00*
Oct-Mar: 11:00-16:00
■ *Adult £5.00, child 5-16yrs £3.00, under 5yrs free, further concessions available*
■ *Halfway between Frensham and Tilford off the A287 Frensham Road.*

Museum of past village life from 1750 to 1960. Set in over 10 acres of garden and woodland and housed in purpose built and reconstructed buildings including a chapel, village hall and cricket pavilion. Historic village playground for over 5's, narrow gauge railway (which operates on Sun), arboretum and woodland walk. All areas accessible by pushchair apart from two of the buildings. Picnic areas. Café will warm baby food and milk on request.

Sherbourne Farm

Shere Road
Albury
Guildford
Surrey GU5 9BW
01483 202586
www.sherbourne-farm.co.uk

■ *Sat-Sun, Bank Holidays, school holidays 10:30-18:00*
■ *Adult £1.75, toddler and over £1.25*
■ *Follow A247 from Woking, then A25 to Dorking, farm on left.*

Working farm with large variety of animals. All areas accessible by pushchair. Will warm milk on request. Parking available at farm or in Silent Pool car park.

Sutton Ecology Centre

The Old Rectory
Festival Walk
Carshalton
Surrey SM5 3NY
020 8770 5820

■ *Park open dawn to dusk. Centre open Sat 10:00-16:30*
■ *Free entry*
■ *Off A232 Carshalton High Street.*

Park and ecology centre with different habitats such as ponds, wetlands and organic. Children's area with frog hopping, mini beasts and pond dipping. Most of paths accessible by pushchair. Runs as school and education centre Mon-Fri and on Sat as information centre and for hiring nets for pond dipping. No café but Heritage Centre next door has tea room. Small car park at centre or pay and display on High Street.

Surrey Society of Model Engineers

At Sutton and East Surrey Water plc site
Mill Lane
Leatherhead
Surrey KT22 9AA
020 8397 3932 (John Cook – correspondence address 27 Vallis Way, Hook, Chessington, Surrey KT9 1PE)

■ *Good Friday-Sep: second Sun in month and Bank Holidays, plus New Years Day, 11:00-16:00*
■ *£1 per ride or 6 rides for £5*
■ *Close to Leatherhead town centre, near junction of Waterway Road and Guildford Road*

Ground level and raised tracks covering over 1 mile, offering passenger rides for anyone who can sit without support. Clubhouse offers refreshments. Parking in dry weather on site, in wet weather in Bull Hill or Station Road car parks, which is a short walk away.

Syon Park

Brentford
Middlesex TW8 8JF
020 8560 0882/020 8560 0881
www.syonpark.co.uk

■ *Daily 10:30-17:30 or dusk for gardens*
■ *Gardens and House: adult £6.95, child 5-16yrs £5.95, Gardens only: adult £3.50, child 5-16yrs £2.20, further concessions available*
■ *From M3 take A316 to Twickenham, turn left to Isleworth, just before Busch Corner turn right into Park Road and follow brown tourist signs.*

The London home of the Duke of

Northumberland is set in 30 acres of Capability Brown parkland and is noted for its 200 species of rare trees. Ornamental lake and 19th Century conservatory. Can picnic in gardens. The Aquatic Experience, London Butterfly House, and Snakes and Ladders (an indoor adventure play-ground) are all on site. Miniature steam railway at extra charge operating some weekends and Bank Holidays. Birthday parties catered for in Snakes and Ladders and Aquatic Experience. All areas are accessible by pushchair. Café. Will warm baby food and milk on request.

Syon Park - The Aquatic Experience

Brentford
Middlesex TW8 8JF
020 8847 4730
www.aquatic-experience.org

■ *Summer: daily 10:00-17:30*
Winter: daily (except Christmas Day, Boxing Day and New Year's Day) 10:00-16:30
■ *Adults £4.00, under 2 yrs free*
■ *From M3 take A316 to Twickenham, turn left to Isleworth, just before Busch Corner turn right into Park Road and follow brown tourist signs.*

Exhibition of rescued and endangered species that live in or near water, especially in rain forest areas. Lecture theatre, dangerous beasts section. No café or toilets in exhibition but can use facilities at patio café at no extra charge. Birthday parties catered for.
P

Syon Park - The London Butterfly House

Syon Park
Brentford
Middlesex TW8 8JF
020 8560 7272
www.butterflies.org.uk

■ *Summer: daily 10:00-17:00*
Winter: daily (except Christmas day and Boxing Day) 10:00-15:30
■ *Adult £4.95, child 3-16yrs £3.95, under 3yrs free, further concessions available*
■ *From M3 take A316 to Twickenham, turn left to Isleworth, just before Busch Corner turn right into Park Road and follow brown tourist signs.*

A covered garden set amongst ponds and water cascades with over 1,000 free flying butterflies, birds and bizarre insects. Gift shop. No café or toilets in butterfly house but can use facilities at patio café at no extra charge. **P**

Syon Park - Snakes and Ladders

Syon Park
Brentford
Middlesex TW8 8JF
020 8847 0946
www.snakes-and-ladders.co.uk

■ *Daily 10:00-18:00, session length is 2 hours*
■ *Children over 5yrs £4.00-£5.00, 2-5yrs £3.00-£4.00, under 2yrs £2.00-£3.00 depending on time*
■ *From M3 take A316 to Twickenham, turn left to Isleworth, just before Busch Corner turn right into Park Road and follow brown tourist signs.*

Three tier adventure play area with intermediate 2-5's area. Separate toddler area. Outdoor adventure play-ground, battery operated motorbikes at extra charge. Coffee shop serving hot and cold snacks. Birthday parties catered for. **P**

Thorpe Park

Staines Road
Chertsey
Surrey KT16 8PN
0870 444 4466

www.thorpepark.co.uk

■ *Apr-Nov: check opening times before travelling*
■ *Adult £27, child under 12yrs £20, under 4yrs free*
■ *On A320 between Chertsey and Staines, follow brown tourist signs.*

Theme park with attractions for younger children such as Thorpe Farm, Octopus Garden (rides and slides), Neptune's Kingdom (sandy beach area with shallow fun pools, water jets and slides) and Canada Creek Railway. All areas accessible by pushchair. Wide range of cafes, restaurants, picnic areas and burger bars. Bottles can be warmed at the medical centre.

Trilakes Animal Park and Fishery

Yateley Road
Sandhurst
Berkshire GU47 8JQ
01252 873191
www.blackwater-valley.org.uk

■ *Apr-Oct: daily 08:00-19:30 or dusk if earlier*
■ *Adult £3, children £2, under 4yrs free*
■ *Yateley Road is off Sandhurst High Street.*

Children's zoo with chipmunks, goats, miniature horses, rabbits, donkeys, pigs and sheep. Site is set in 18 acres of picturesque lakes. Can hand feed some of the animals. Remote control boating pond, model railway and mouse house. All areas accessible by pushchair. Café.

Waltham Place Organic Gardens

Church Hill
White Waltham
Maidenhead
Berkshire SL6 3JH
01628 825517
www.walthamplace.com
estateoffice@walthamplace.com

■ *Apr-end Sep: Mon-Fri 10:00-16:00 closed Bank Holiday Mondays*
■ *Adults £3.50, children £2*
■ *Exit Junction 8/9 on M4, then A404(M) following signs for White Waltham. Estate is on left past church.*

Extensive 40 acres with landscaped gardens, ornamental vegetable gardens, kitchen garden and rare breed animals. All areas accessible by pushchair. Tearoom and shop selling organic produce.

Watercress Line

Information Office
The Railway Station
Alresford
Hampshire SO24 9JH
01962 733810 (General Information)
01962 734866 (Talking Timetable)
www.watercressline.co.uk

■ *May-Sep: Tue-Sun, Oct-Apr: Sat-Sun*
■ *Adult £7.50 return, child 3-16yrs £3.50 return, under 3yrs free, special rates for special events*
■ *Alresford and Alton stations are signposted off A31.*

Mid-Hants steam railway offering steam train trips. Special events throughout the year such as Day with Thomas, footplate excursion, Christmas specials. Ropley station and Alresford station have picnic areas. Children's play area, shop and disabled facitlies at Ropley station. Parking is pay and display.

Weald and Downland Open Air Museum

Singleton
Chichester
West Sussex PO18 0EU
01243 811363
www.wealddown.co.uk
office@wealddown.co.uk

■ *Mar-end Oct: daily 10:30-18:00*
Nov- end Feb: Sat-Sun 10:30-16:00 plus every day of Feb half term
26th Dec to 1st Jan: daily 10:30-16:00
■ *Adult £7.50, child 5-15yrs £4, under 5yrs free*
■ *North of Chichester on A286.*
Museum consisting of nearly 50 historic buildings dating from 13th to 19th Century, many with period gardens, together with farm animals, woodland walks and a picturesque lake. Working Tudor kitchen, working water mill and heavy horses at work. Most areas accessible by pushchair, although may need to leave outside some of houses. Tea room which will warm baby food and milk on request. Lots of space to run around and special events time-tabled throughout year.

Whipsnade Wild Animal Park

Dunstable
Bedfordshire LU6 2LF
01582 872171
www.whipsnade.co.uk

■ *Mar-Oct: daily 10:00-18:00*
Nov-Jan: daily 10:00-closing time varies throughout rest of year (closed Christmas)
■ *Adult £13.50, child 3-15yrs £10.10, under 3yrs free, further concessions available, parking £3.00, to take car into park £10.00*
■ *From A5 onto B4540 Common Road.*
Wildlife conservation park set in 600 acres of parkland. It is home to more than 2,500 animals including elephants, giraffes, bears, tigers, rhinos and hippos. Daily demonstrations and talks. Walk, drive or take free safari bus round park. All areas are accessible by push-chair except hedgerow walk which has bark chippings. Several cafes serving range of food including children's menu. Microwave available in Café on the Lake for warming baby food and milk. Picnic areas. Playgrounds for younger and older children.

Witley Centre

Haslemere Road
Witley
Godalming
Surrey GU8 5PX
01428 604823
witleycentre@nationaltrust.org.uk

■ *Common open all year. Centre open end Mar-beg Nov: Tue-Fri 11:00-16:00, Sat-Sun and Bank Holiday Mondays 11:00-17:00*
■ *Free entry (donations accepted)*
■ *Take exit for Milford from A3 and follow signs. Off A286 between Milford and Brook.*
Purpose built visitor education centre surrounded by mix of woodland and heath in which there are plenty of country walks and cycle rides. All areas accessible by pushchair although some of common is quite sandy. Café and picnic areas. **P**

Woking Miniature Railway

Botany Barns Garden Centre
Barrs Lane
Knaphill
Woking
Surrey GU21 2JW
07952 907667
www.wmrs.co.uk
wmrs@bigfoot.com

■ *Easter-end Sep: Sun and season specials*
Miniature railway with special events such as Teddy Bear's Picnic, Mother's Day. Station building and engine sheds, picnic area and shop selling drinks and 'Thomas' items. **P**

PLAYGROUNDS

Addlestone

Victory Park Play Area
Surrey KT15 2AX

■ *From Addlestone High street, follow brown signs down Victory Park Road.*
Swings, baby swings, slides, climbing frame, see-saw, wooden animals. Enclosed playground with benches and situated in large playing field. Paddling pool open May to Sep. Toilets locked when playground was researched. **P**

Brookwood

Connaught Crescent Playground
Surrey GU24 0AW

■ *From Connaught Road coming from Woking, turn right into Connaught Crescent, turn right at fork. Pathway on right after number 79 leads to playground.*
Swings, baby swings, slide, spring rockers. Enclosed playground with bench. Parking requires a voucher from 13:00-14:00. **P**

Burpham

Glendale Drive
Guildford
Surrey GU4 7HX

■ *From A320 turn left at Clay Lane in Jacob's Well. At Sainsbury's roundabout turn right, then left at next roundabout into New Inn Lane. Turn left into Glendale Drive. Park is hidden behind houses so can be hard to find.*
Swing, baby swings, slide, climbing frame. Parking is on road a short walk down track. **P**

Burpham

Sutherland Memorial Playground
Clay Lane
Guildford
Surrey GU4 7PF

■ *From Woking on A3100, turn right at Sainsbury's roundabout.*
Swings, baby swings, slides, climbing frames, adventure playground type construction with rope bridges. Enclosed playground with benches and separate fenced off area within playground for younger children. Toilets in nearby sports hall or in Sainsbury's. **P**

Byfleet

Sanway Road Play area
Surrey KT14 7SF

■ *Turn off High Road in Byfleet into Rectory Lane and follow road around to left, after which there is a turn into Sanway Road.*
Swings, baby swings, slide, spring rockers. Enclosed playground with bench. **P**

Chertsey

Chertsey Recreational Ground
Guildford Road
Surrey KT16 9BW

■ *On A320 from Woking, go under M25 and recreational ground is on left just before roundabout leading to trading estate.*
Swings, baby swings, slides, climbing frame, roundabout, see-saw, spring rocker, rocket. Lots of grassy areas to play on, benches and paddling pool open May to Sep. **P**

Chertsey

Gogmore Farm Park
Riversdell Close
Surrey KT16 9JW

■ *On A320 from Woking follow signs to town centre as far as the roundabout just before the centre where Gogmore Farm Park is signposted to the left.*
Swings, baby swings, slides, climbing frames, maze, wooden animals, 'death slide'. Enclosed playground with benches and separate toddler area within playground. Large grassy area, stream nearby. Parking on road or pay and display. **P**

Chertsey
The Orchard and Abbeyfield
Staines Lane
Surrey KT16 8PS

■ *Take A320 from Woking to Chertsey; follow signs to Staines continuing on A320. Turn right at Twynersh roundabout into Staines Lane.*
Swings, baby swings, slides, climbing frame. Large playing fields and benches. A few on-road parking spaces. **P**

Cobham
Cobham Recreation Ground
Oakdene Road
Surrey KT11 2LL

■ *Follow signs to Cobham from A3 or through Byfleet. At roundabout in Cobham, turn left onto Between Streets and Oakdene Road is first on left.*
Swings, baby swings, slides, climbing frames, spring rockers, roundabout. Large playing fields and benches. **P**

East Horsley
Kingston Meadows
Kingston Avenue
Surrey KT24 6QT

■ *From A246 Epsom Road, turn left into Ockham Road and then left again into Kingston Avenue.*
Baby swings, slide, climbing frame. Grassy area and bench. **P**

Goldsworth Park
Goldwater Lodge Play Area
Woking
Surrey GU21 3QR

■ *Halfway round lake from Waitrose or by road, turn off Lockfield Drive into Kirkland Avenue and follow signs to Goldwater Lodge.*
Swings, baby swings, slide, climbing frames, 'death slide', spinner, spring rockers. Enclosed playground with benches. Skate park, fields and basketball courts nearby. **P**

Goldsworth Park
Lakeview Recreation Ground
Woking
Surrey GU21 3AR

■ *From Lockfield Drive, turn into Marston Road. Turn right into Sythwood and playground is on right.*
Swings, baby swings, slides, climbing frames, spinner, spring rockers. Enclosed playground with benches. Parking is in lay-bys on road outside. **P**

Goldsworth Park
Lidstone Close Play Area
Woking
Surrey GU21 3BG

■ *From Lockfield Drive turn into Marston Road. Lidstone Close is at end of Marston Road.*
Baby swings, slide. Very small playground. Limited on street parking. **P**

Goldsworth Park
Millennium Place Play Area
Woking
Surrey GU21 6DP

■ *Off Vale Farm Road.*
Baby swings, spring rocker. bench. Small playground. **P**

Goldsworth Park
Waitrose Play Area
Woking
Surrey GU21 3LG

■ *From Lockfield Drive, turn right into Bampton Way; turn left into Denton Way and right into Waitrose car park.*
Slide, climbing frame. Play area is in forecourt in front of shops and is not enclosed by fencing. Benches. **P**

Guildford
Guildford Castle
Castle street
Guildford
Surrey GU2 5BB

01483 444702 (Parks Department)
www.ukattraction.com/south-east-england/guildford-castle.htm

■ *From Guildford High Street going up the hill, turn right into Chapel Street and left into Castle Street.*

Norman stone mote and bailey fortress surrounded by beautiful gardens. No playground equipment, but children are welcome in the grounds. Parking is on road or in Guildford town centre car parks.

Guildford

Stoke Park
Stoke Road
Surrey GU1 4HW

■ *On A320 from Woking to Guildford.*

Swings, baby swings, slide, climbing frame. Benches. Duck pond nearby and kiosk to buy snacks/drinks. Paddling pool nearby. Putting, tennis courts, grassy areas. Parking on roads nearby can be difficult. **P**

Horsell

Horsell Moor Play Area
Brewery Road
Woking
Surrey GU21 4LP

■ *Follow Brewery Road away from Woking towards Horsell. Playground is on left just before Horsell cricket pavilion.*

Swings, baby swings, slide, climbing frame, fireman's pole. Enclosed play area with bench. Can be busy just after school finishes. Parking is voucher parking and quite limited.

Horsell

High Street Play Area
Woking
Surrey GU21 4SY

■ *Follow Brewery Road away from Woking towards Horsell and into Horsell High Street. Playground is on right before shops.*

Swing, baby swing, slide, climbing frame, spring rockers, roundabout, balancing beams, hide and seek frames. Small enclosed play area with benches. Can be busy just after school finishes. Parking is limited on road. **P**

Horsell

Queen Elizabeth Gardens Formal Park
High Street
Woking
Surrey GU21 4SY

■ *Follow Brewery Road away from Woking towards Horsell and into Horsell High Street. Gardens are on the right.*

Planted garden areas, grassy area and benches. **P**

Horsell

Wheatsheaf Common Play Area
Woking
Surrey GU21 4AL

■ *Take Chobham Road from Woking towards Chobham. Playground is on right opposite Wheatsheaf pub.*

Swings, baby swings, slides, climbing frame. Grassy area and woodland areas nearby. Benches. Parking very limited or voucher parking.

Knaphill

Cavell Way Play Area
Woking
Surrey GU21 2TJ

■ *From Woking head onto Lockfield Drive and then onto Redding Way, follow road round and eventually turn left into Cavell Way. Playground is immediately on left.*

Swings, baby swings, slide, climbing frame, roundabout, see-saw, spring rocker. New playground suitable for older and younger children. Parking on road. **P**

Knaphill

Cubitt Way Play Area
Woking
Surrey GU21 2QJ

■ *From Woking head onto Lockfield Drive and then onto Redding Way, turn right into Cubitt Way.*
Swings, baby swings, slide, climbing frame.

Knaphill
Percheron Drive Play Area
Woking
Surrey GU21 2QY

■ *From Woking head onto Lockfield Drive and then onto Redding Way, at roundabout take third exit for Percheron Drive.*
Swing, baby swing, slide, climbing frame, spring rockers.

Knaphill
Southwood Avenue Play Area
Woking
Surrey GU21 2EZ

■ *From Woking go towards Aldershot along Lockfield Drive. After third round-about, once in Hermitage Road, take second right into Inkerman Road. Take first left into Northwood Avenue and first left again into Southwood Avenue. Playground is round the bend on the left.*
Swing, baby swings, slide, see-saw, spring rockers. Enclosed play ground with benches. Parking on road. **P**

Knaphill
Strathcona Gardens Play Area
Woking
Surrey GU21 2AZ

■ *From Woking head onto Lockfield Drive and then onto Redding Way, turn left into Strathcona Gardens.*
Swings, baby swings, slide, climbing frame, see-saw, spring rocker. New playground suitable for older and younger children.

Knaphill
Sussex Road Play Area
Woking
Surrey GU21 2RA

■ *From Knaphill High Street head in direction of A322. Turn left into Sussex Road and turn right into small driveway about halfway down.*
Swings, baby swings, slide, climbing frame, spring rockers. Small enclosed playground. **P**

Knaphill
Waterers Park Play Area
Barley Mow Lane
Woking
Surrey GU21 2HT

■ *From Woking head towards Knaphill up Anchor Hill. Pass Barr's Lane and take next right into Barley Mow Lane.*
Swings, baby swings, slide, climbing frame. Small enclosed playground situated in middle of large playing field.

Maybury
Alpha Road Play Area
Woking
Surrey GU22 8EJ

■ *Head towards Maybury on Oriental Road. Turn left at Maybury Hill and immediately right into Princess Road. Alpha Road is third on left.*
Swings, baby swings, climbing frames, see-saw, spring rockers. Grassy area. **P**

Maybury
Boundary Road Recreation Area
Woking
Surrey GU21 5BS

■ *Turn left from Chertsey Road on northern approach just before Woking town centre. Playground is next to Basingstoke canal.*
Swings, baby swing, slides, climbing frame. Small enclosed playground with bench. Skate board ramps nearby. Parking is voucher parking.

Mayford
Saunders Lane
Woking
Surrey GU22 0NN

■ *Take A320 from Woking towards Guildford. At Mayford roundabout turn right into Smarts Heath Road and then right into Saunders Lane. Playground is not visible from road but is next to village hall.*
Swing, baby swing, see-saw, spring rockers, roundabout, balancing beams. Small enclosed play area with bench. **P**

New Haw
Heathervale Recreation Ground
Woodham Road
Surrey KT15 3AP

■ *From Six Ways Roundabout take A245 Woodham Lane. Go straight over roundabout in village. Heathervale Road is fourth turning on right.*
Swings, baby swings, slides, climbing frame, see-saw, spring rockers, wooden horses. Large enclosed playground with grassy area, benches and paddling pool open May-Sep. Multi-use games area and skating facilities. Toilets locked when playground was researched. 🚻 **P**

New Haw
Woodham Lodge
Amis Avenue
Surrey KT15 3ET

■ *Follow A245 Woodham Lane to New Haw. From Six Ways Roundabout. Turn left at roundabout in village. Turn left again into Amis Road.*
Baby swings, slides, climbing frames, see-saw. Enclosed playground with small grassy area and benches. Parking in day centre or on road. **P**

Old Woking
Rydens Way Recreational Ground
Woking
Surrey GU22 9DG

■ *From Old Woking Road head towards Maybury, turn left into Gloucester Road. Turn right at end of road into Rydens Way. Playground is at end of road in middle of grass.*
Swings, baby swings, slide, climbing frame, horse, motorbike. Small enclosed playground. **P**

Ottershaw
Foxhills Road Play Area
Surrey KT16 0NQ

■ *Take A320 from Woking towards Chertsey. Turn left at Ottershaw roundabout and immediately right into Foxhills Road. Playground is a little way down road on left.*
Swings, baby swings, slides, climbing frame, maze, see-saw, roundabout. Playing fields with wooded area and benches. Multi-use games area and skating facilities for older children. 🚻 **P**

Pirbright
Pirbright Village Green
Surrey GU24 0BL

■ *Follow signs towards Aldershot from Woking along A324 Lockfield Drive and Hermitage Road. At crossroads turn left and then immediately right into Cemetery Pales. Playground is next to Lord Pirbright's Hall on village green.*
Swings, baby swings, slide, see-saw, roundabout, rocking horse. Enclosed playground with park and duck pond next to play area. **P**

Pyrford
Pyrford Common Road Play Area
Surrey GU22 8UD

■ *Turn off Old Woking Road into Pyrford Common Road. Playground is on right.*
Swings, baby swings, slides, climbing frames, spring rockers, see-saw, play boards. Enclosed play area with benches. Large grassy area and woodland walks. **P**

Ripley
Ripley Common Playground
Surrey GU23 6AN

■ *Head towards Ripley. Playground is just off High Street, on Ripley Common next to*

cricket pitch.
Swings, baby swings, slide, climbing frames, spring rockers, see-saw, roundabout. Enclosed play area with bench. Grassy area. **P**

Send
Send Road Play Area
Surrey GU23 7HN

■ *Take A247 from Old Woking towards Send. Playground is on right in village.*
Swings, baby swings, slide, climbing frame, spring rocker, see-saw. Enclosed play area with benches set within large playing field. **P**

Sheerwater
Sheerwater Recreation Ground
Blackmore Crescent
Woking
Surrey GU21 5NW

■ *Follow Boundary Road or Walton Road away from Town Centre. Cross over Monument Road into Eve Road. Turn left into Albert Drive and, after business park, left again into Blackmore Crescent. Near end of road turn left at small signpost for Athletics Track.*
Swings, baby swings, slide, climbing frames, see-saw, roundabout, spring rockers. Enclosed play area with benches set within large enclosed grassy area. **P**

St John's
St Johns' Lakeside Play Area
Batten Avenue
Woking
Surrey GU21 8TP

■ *Follow A324 St John's Road, turn right at first mini roundabout and straight on at second. Follow Hermitage Road past Winston Churchill School and take first left into Amis Road. Batten Avenue is off Amis Road.*
Swing, baby swing, slide, climbing frame, spring rocker, see-saw. Parking on road. **P**

St John's
St John's Lye
Woking
Surrey GU21 7SJ

■ *In middle of St. John's village turn into car park opposite Alldays. Playground is on the Green.*
Swings, baby swings, slide, climbing frame, see-saw, roundabout, spring rockers. Enclosed playground situated in middle of playing field.

Slyfield
Parsons Green
Guildford
Surrey GU1 1QY

■ *Follow A320 to Guildford. At roundabout in Bellfields turn left and follow Bellfields Road round to left, Parsons Green is on the right.*
Swings, baby swings, slide, climbing frame, spring rocker. Parking on road. **P**

Slyfield
Waterside Road
Guildford
Surrey GU1 1RE

■ *Follow A320 to Guildford. At roundabout in Bellfields, turn left onto Woking Road, then first right onto Waterside Road.*
Swings, baby swings, slides, climbing frames, rocket, spring rockers. Parking on road. **P**

Stoke D'Abernon
Stoke Recreation Ground
Evelyn Way
Stoke D'Abernon
Surrey KT11 2SJ

■ *Head towards Ripley, then towards Ockham and then towards Stoke D'Abernon. Just before going over railway bridge, turn left into Blundel Lane. Turn sharp right into Evelyn Way.*
Swings, slide, climbing frame. Benches. **P**

Sutton Green

Foxes Path Recreation Ground
Woking
Surrey GU4 7QY

■ *Take A320 towards Guildford and turn left into Whitmoor Lane. At T-junction turn left into Sutton Green Road. Turn right at tight bend, then immediately right again into Foxes Path. Playground is on left.*
Swing, baby swing, slide, climbing frame, roundabout. Enclosed playground with benches. Limited parking on road. **P**

West Byfleet

Camphill Road
Surrey KT14 6EF

■ *Take Old Woking Road towards West Byfleet past Waitrose and turn left into Camphill Road. Playground is on right next to school.*
Swings, baby swings, slides, climbing frames, roundabout, see-saw, spring rocker. Enclosed play area with benches. Large grassy area adjacent. Parking is limited on road. **P**

Westfield

Bonsey Lane Play Area
Woking
Surrey GU22 9PP

■ *From Westfield Road turn into Bonsey Lane.*
Swings, baby swings, slide, climbing frame, spring rocker. Small enclosed playground within recreational area. Parking limited. **P**

Westfield

Westfield Common Play Area
Woking
Surrey GU22 9PD

■ *From Westfield Road, turn into Balfour Avenue and then left into Willow Bank.*
Swings, slide, climbing frame, rope ladder. Small enclosed playground with benches situated by small playing field and pond. **P**

Weybridge

Churchfield Recreation Ground
Churchfield Road
Surrey KT13 8DB

■ *From A320, follow signs to Weybridge on A317. At junction with B3121 take second exit signposted Weybridge, turn right onto Churchfield Road*
Swings, baby swings, slides, climbing frames, sand pit, wooden train, see-saw, spring rockers. Large grassy area, benches and paddling pool. Parking is pay and display.

Weybridge

Oatlands Recreation Ground
Barham Close
Oatlands Drive
Surrey KT13 9RR

■ *From A245, follow signs to Weybridge. At Hanger Hill, take 2nd mini roundabout along Oatlands Drive. Barham Close is fourth road on right.*
Swings, baby swings, slides, climbing frames, roundabout, spring rockers, 'death slide'. Large grassy area and benches. Parking limited. **P**

Woking

DeLara Way Play Area
Woking
Surrey GU21 6NY

■ *From Goldsworth Road, turn into Kingsway. DeLara Way is halfway up on left. Playground is on right.*
Swing, baby swing, slide, see-saw. Enclosed playground with benches that is quite run down and difficult to get buggy up steep grass verge to the equipment. **P**

Woking
Loop Road Recreational Ground
Woking
Surrey GU22 9BQ

■ *From Kingfield Road or Westfield Road turn into Loop Road.*

Swings, baby swings, slides, climbing frame, horse. **P**

Woking
Woking Park Playground
Kingfield Road
Woking
Surrey GU22 9BA

■ *From Woking follow signs to Leisure Centre and Pool in the Park.*

Swings, baby swings, slides, climbing frame, roundabout, train, bridge and tunnel, spring rockers. Large enclosed area suitable for younger and older children. Benches. Park nearby. Toilets in Leisure Centre. **P**

WALKS AND WOODLANDS

Box Hill (National Trust)
National Trust Information Centre
Box Hill Road
Tadworth
Surrey KT20 7LB
01306 888793 (info & shops)
01306 885502 (warden)
www.nationaltrust.org.uk

■ *Summer: daily 09:00–17:00*
Winter: daily 11:00–16:00

■ *Car park £2.00, free entry into park*

■ *Near Dorking at the A24 Burford Bridge roundabout, follow signs for Mickleham and turn right into a zigzag road.*

Country Park with views, walks through woods and chalk downland. Rising 400 feet from River Mole. Viewpoint accessible by gravel path but some walks are steep or bumpy, thus limited access to pushchairs and wheel chairs. Shop with plant sales. Information Centre. Servery for take away snacks and drinks and will provide heating facility for baby food. The Donkey Green is an open grassy area suitable for picnics. Special events organised e.g. Country Fair in Summer, children's activity afternoons in school holidays and Discovery Days for families in May and October. Also Easter Egg Hunt organised. Booking required for events–01306 742809.

Chatley Heath & Semaphore Tower
Old Lane
Effingham
Surrey
01932 862762 (Recorded Information)
01372 458822

■ *6 months in Summer: Mon, Sat and Sun 12:00–17:00*
Winter: some Sundays
Wed during Surrey school holidays

■ *Free entry but exhibitions cost adults £2.00, children £1.50, under 6yrs free*

■ *Travelling south on A3 take M25 junction 10 turn-off but continue south on slip road as if going back on A3 and follow signs for Effingham.*

A 15 minute walk through woods to tower which is a unique ex-Admiralty Naval Station with well-marked trails. It formed a chain with other towers to signal messages between Admiralty in Whitehall and Portsmouth. Pushchair and wheelchair access difficult and it is a rough sandy terrain, but safe parking for buggies available. Shop & country-side Information Centre. Café in Boldermere car park that will warm baby food and milk on request. Special events organised e.g. Teddy Bears' picnic in July, Father Christmas in December. Open for special visits by arrangement. Lectures available.
P

Chobham Common

01483 401880
07968 832502 (Mobile in emergency only)

■ *Open daily*
■ *Free entry*
■ *North of Chobham on the B386 towards Sunningdale. Car park at roundabout or on B386.*

Mainly heathland with occasional trees. 1500 acres of open space. Three types of heather can be found plus rare plants and animals. Several public footpaths cross the area. Double buggy and wheelchair access when dry. **P**

Claremont Landscape Garden (National Trust)

Portsmouth Road
Esher
Surrey KT10 9JG
01372 469421
www.nationaltrust.org.uk/claremont

■ *Apr-Oct: Mon-Fri 10:00–18:00, Sat-Sun and Bank Holidays 10:00-19:00*
Nov-Mar: Tue-Sun 10:00-dusk
■ *Adult £4.00, child £2.00, under 5yrs free. Free entry to NT members*
■ *Off the A307 south-west of Esher.*

English landscape garden. Picturesque lake and island, grotto, turf amphitheatre. Wildfowl to feed (bird food available from kiosk). Steep paths but also level pathway around lake and a children's trail. Tea room (restricted opening hours in Winter). Highchairs and half portions available; staff in tea room will heat baby food on request. There is also a children's area with books and colouring. Can picnic in grounds. No dogs between April and end October. For details of the various children's activities also available during school holidays phone the enquiry line. **P**

Frensham Common

01252 792416 (Ranger's office)
www.waverley.gov.uk

■ *Daily 09:00–21:00*
■ *Free entry except Summer weekends when cost is £2.50 per car*
■ *5 miles south of Farnham, split across the A287.*

Two ponds in almost 1000 acres of common lowland heath popular for angling. Ponds and common used for recreation and conservation; Frensham Great Pond good for paddling and has small yachting club. Several signed walks start at the Information Room at the Great Pond, including a short easier access loop for wheelchair users. Cycle routes. Double buggy and wheelchair access in parts. Picnic area by Great Pond. Café open all year (10:00 to 18:00 depending on season). It offers refreshments and will warm baby food and milk on request. Various car parks – Pond Lane car park for the Great Pond. **P**

Homewood Country Park

Stonehill Road
Chertsey
Surrey
01932 425715
07870 831340 (mobile)

■ *Open daily*
■ *Free entry*
■ *Off the A320 from Woking to Chertsey, past St Peter's hospital, turn left at mini-roundabout into Holloway Hill. Turn left again into Stonehill Road.*

Country Park within grounds of Botleys Mansion (not open to public). Woodland, lakes, footpath, bridleway and nature trail. Picnic tables and benches. Paths accessible to pushchairs but some areas of nature trail rough. Narrow entrance not suitable for large vehicles.
P

Horsell Common

Shores Road
Woking
Surrey
0860 712503 (warden's mobile)

■ *Open daily*
■ *Free entry*
■ *Car park off the A245 Shores Road, which is off the Six Crossroads roundabout.*

Heathland common and woodland. Large sandpit area and network of paths. Double buggy and wheelchair access but some paths are rough.

Horton Country Park

Horton Lane
Epsom
Surrey KT19 8PL
01372 741191

■ *Daily 09:00-dusk (except Christmas Day and New Year's Day)*
■ *Free entry*
■ *Horton Lane is off the B280 Oxshott-Epsom Road.*

200 acres of meadow and woodland. Picnic area adjoins car park. Details on internet via Borough Council's website. BBQ facilities available for hire but phone beforehand (01372 732462). Events held throughout year.

Leith Hill

Coldharbour
Dorking
Surrey
01306 711777

■ *Woodland & Estate open daily*
Tower open Apr-Sep: Wed, Sat-Sun and Bank Holidays 10:00–17:00
Oct-Mar: Sat-Sun 10:00–15:30
■ *Free entry but car park by rhododendron wood £2 or free parking along road at foot of hill*
Tower costs adult £1.50, child £0.75
■ *From A25 to Dorking, turn right into Hollow Lane after Abinger Hammer. Turn left into Leith Hill Road, and follow road to left into Mosses Wood Road. Tower is on left.*

Highest point in South-East England. 18th Century gothic tower at summit. Woodland with paths but not suitable for pushchairs. Circular trail guides available at £1. Rhododendron wood with accessible paths for pushchairs and wheelchairs. Light refreshments when tower is open or picnic areas by tower and in rhododendron wood.

Lightwater Country Park

The Avenue
Lightwater
Surrey GU18 5RG
01276 479582 (Ranger's Office)
www.surreyheath.gov.uk/tourism - follow link to parks & countryside

■ *Park open daily*
Visitors Centre open Apr-Dec: Sundays and Bank Holidays 11:00-17:00
School holidays: Tue- Fri 12:00-17:00
Also open for group bookings and special events, e.g. birthdays
■ *Free entry*
■ *Off A322 Guildford to Bagshot Road at Lightwater.*

Heathland, woodland, wildflower meadows, bogs and ponds. Paths accessible by pushchairs but some are rough. 'Easy Access Trail' designed for wheelchairs. Picnic tables and Visitors Centre serves snacks.

Newlands Corner

Albury Downs
Surrey

■ *Open daily*
■ *Free entry*
■ *Off A25 east of Guildford.*

Beauty spot with views across Surrey. Walks in woodland and open country-side. Countryside Centre. One easy access trail for pushchairs; other trails may not be suitable. Disabled buggy available for free hire on Sundays. Snack bar for refreshments.

The Pride of the Valley Sculpture Park

Jumps Road
Churt
Farnham
Surrey GU10 2LE
01428 605453
07831 500506 (mobile)
www.thesculpturepark.com
eddiepowell@thesculpturepark.co.uk

- *Tue-Sun, 10:00-17:00 and Bank Holidays*
- *Adult £4.50, Children 5-16yrs £2, under 5yrs free*

1.5 miles of all-weather pathway around lakes, rivers and through woodland, most of which is accessible to wheelchairs and buggies. Sculptures are available to purchase. Children need to be supervised as sculptures should not be used for playing on. The Pride of the Valley Hotel opposite has parking, toilet and refreshment facilities (but is not part of the Sculpture Park). P

Puttenham Common

Suffield Lane
01483 728159

- *Open daily*
- *Free entry*
- *Off A31, one and a half miles south-west of Puttenham along Suffield Lane.*

Heathland, woodland and ponds with several marked trails, some suitable for pushchairs. Picnic area. P

Richmond Park

Holly Lodge
Richmond Park
Richmond
Surrey TW10 5HS
020 8948 3209
Richmond@royalparks.gsi.gov.uk

- *Open daily until dusk*
- *Free entry*
- *From M3, continue on to A316. Old Deer Park is on left after going over River Thames, head right on to A307 to Kingston to locate Richmond Park.*

Largest open space in London including grassland, wetland, woodland and parkland. Fallow and red deer roam the park. Bike hire available (0800 0138000). Park includes Isabella Plantation with large display of flowers. Refreshments available at Pembroke Lodge Cafeteria, Roehampton Pavilion or at Kiosks at all main car parks. Variety of activities also available for children in July and August (contact Park Office for information). P

Runnymede Pleasure Grounds

Windsor Road
Egham
Surrey TW20 0AE
01932 425688
www.visitsurrey.com

- *Mon-Fri 08:00-dusk, Sat-Sun 09:00-dusk*
- *Free but charge for parking*

Large park and garden on River Thames. Play equipment, café, children's rides plus paddling pool in Summer. Covered outdoor tables at café. Picnic tables.

St Martha's Hill

Halfpenny Lane
Guildford
Surrey

- *Open daily*
- *Free*
- *Take the A246 Guildford to Epsom road from Guildford and turn right into Tangier Road. Turn left at T-junction into Warren Road and follow road round sharp right-hand bend to reach crossroads. Halfpenny Lane is straight on at crossroads.*

Short, steady climb up sandy path to small Norman Church at top of St Martha's Hill, on the route of the North Downs Way. Superb views. Woodland. Pushchairs not recommended. Small grassy area near car park. **P**

The Sheepleas

West Horsley

■ *Open daily*
■ *Free*
■ *South of the A246 Guildford to Epsom road; take the Shere Road turning at the small roundabout on the A246 at West Horsley. Two car parks: Shere Road and Green Dene.*

Woodland walks in a 270 acre site on the chalk slopes of the North Downs, lying within the Surrey Hills Area of Outstanding Beauty. Beech and oak woodland, hazel scrub and rich wildflower meadow. Site of Special Scientific Interest (SSSI). Double buggy and wheelchair access but can be muddy. **P**

Silent Pool

Near Shere
Surrey

■ *Open daily*
■ *Free*
■ *On the A25 Guildford-Dorking road, 1 mile east of Newlands Corner.*

Tree-encircled pool with paths leading onto North Downs Way. Fence protecting walkers from water most of the time. Walk around pool takes 10-15 minutes. Several much longer walks possible but pushchair and wheelchair access around pool only. **P**

The Vyne (National Trust)

Sherborne St John
Basingstoke
Hampshire RG24 9HL
01256 881337

■ *24th Mar-31st Oct: Wed–Sun and Bank Holiday Mondays, Grounds 12:30–17:30 and Estate 13:30–17:30*
■ *Grounds and estate adult £7.00, child £3.50, Grounds only adult £4.00, child £2.00, under 5yrs free, family tickets and other concessions available*
■ *4 miles north of Basingstoke on the A340.*

Nearly 500 acres of woodland garden, walks and views. Double buggy and wheelchair access around grounds. Early 16th Century house. Shop. Restaurant/tea room with highchairs. Grassy verges and tables for picnics around the car park. Special events: outdoor theatre performance in August, Easter Egg Trail, Butterfly Walk and Sticky Autumn Walk. Telephone for details. **P**

Wellington Country Park

Riseley
Near Reading
Berkshire RG7 1SP
01189 326444

■ *Beg Mar-end Oct: daily 10:00–17:30*
■ *Adult £4.80, child £2.50, under 5yrs free, plus other concessions available*
■ *Off the A33 south of Reading between Reading and Basingstoke, or well signposted from junction 11 off the M4.*

Country park with campsite. Boating, crazy golf, mini railway, adventure playground (age 6 yrs upwards), children's animal farm, nature trails. Gift shop, café and coffee shop serving small portions for children. Picnic and BBQ areas (BBQ available to hire). **P**

Whitmoor, Rickford and Stringer's Commons

Worplesdon

■ *Open daily*
■ *Free*
■ *Between the A320 and A322.*

Small car park near Britten's Pond which is off Salt Box Road.

Three commons of woodland and heath with a network of paths. Whitmoor and Rickford Commons have been designated Sites of Special Scientific Interest, and have marked tracks for walks of different lengths. Start at the car park to the rear of the Jolly Farmer on Burdenshott Road (off A320 Woking to Guildford Road). Stringer's Common is more wooded and on the edge is Britten's Pond used by anglers. Broadstreet and Backside Commons form part of the Worplesdon Commons and are off the A323 Aldershot Road. There is also a short circular walk suitable for pushchairs and wheelchairs. **P**

Windsor Great Park – Savill Garden

Wick Lane
Englefield Green
Egham
Surrey
01753 847518 (Crown Estate Office)

■ *Mar-Oct: daily 10:00–18:00*
Nov-Feb: daily 10:00–16:00
(except Christmas Day and Boxing Day)

■ *Apr to May adults £5.50, child £2.50, Jun to Oct adult £4.50, child £1.50, Nov to Mar adult £3.50, child £1.25, under 5yrs free. Car park free if paying entrance fee*

■ *M25 Junction 13, off the A30 and clearly signposted from Ascot, Bagshot, Egham, Windsor and Old Windsor.*

Woodland garden created by Sir Eric Savill within the grounds of historic Windsor Great Park. Shop and restaurant with highchairs and range of hot and cold snacks and cakes. No dogs allowed. **P**

Windsor Great Park – Valley Gardens

Wick Road
Englefield Green
Egham
Surrey
01753 847518 (Crown Estate Office)

■ *Daily 08:00–18:00*

■ *Free entry but car park charges £4.00, rising to £5.50 during Apr, May and Oct (car park barrier only accepts 10p, 50p and £1.00 coins)*

■ *Off the A30 – follow signs for Savill Garden which is half a mile to the west. Enter car park by a gate in Wick Road.*

Woodland garden situated on the north bank of Virginia Water Lake within the eastern boundary of Windsor Great Park.

Windsor Great Park–Virginia Water

Near Sunningdale
Surrey
01753 847518 (Crown Estate Office)

■ *Daily 07:30-dusk*

■ *Free entry but car park charges £4.00*

■ *On the A30 from Sunningdale heading towards Egham.*

Half a mile of artificial lake in woodland. Rhododendrons and azaleas. Totem pole. Café. Good for picnics.

Winkworth Arboretum (National Trust)

Hascombe Road
Godalming
Surrey GU8 4AD
01483 208477
www.nationaltrust.org.uk

■ *Daily dawn-dusk*

■ *Adult £4.00, child £2.00 plus family tickets available. Free entry to NT members*

■ *Follow A3100 to Godalming. In Godalming, turn left onto B2130 Brighton Road. Car park is on left or further car park on Thorncombe street.*

Hillside woodland. Over 1300 different trees and shrubs; stunning autumn colours. Not all paths accessible to pushchairs due to steep steps but some level walks available. Café within the shop is closed Mon-Tue and has some further seasonal variation. **P**

Eating out

THIS CHAPTER is not an exhaustive list of every eating and drinking establishment in Woking and the surrounding area but it is a guide to the places that will welcome children and have the facilities that will help to make the experience of eating out with your children, a more relaxing and enjoyable one. We've identified the most important facilities such as high chairs, play areas, children's menus, non smoking areas and willingness to heat milk or food but as with everything in life, things change so be sure to ring ahead if you want be certain that the establishment still offers a particular facility.

Most cafes and restaurants have a non smoking area so we have only identified the pubs and some restaurants that do or don't have a non smoking area. We have only described the children's menu if it includes food other than burgers, nuggets and chips.

We've organised this chapter according to geographical location, starting with the Food Court in the Peacocks shopping centre, we then move on to other establishments within Woking town centre and the final section contains places in the surrounding area and villages.

Happy Eating !

FOOD COURT

All the establishments in the Food Court have shared facilities such as toilets, disabled toilets and baby changing. None of the establishments have free parking so you need to park in one of the town centre car parks.

Aroma

Lower Concourse
The Peacocks
Woking
Surrey GU21 1GB
01483 714159

■ *Mon-Sat 09:30-18:00, Sun 10:00-17:00*
Café serving sandwiches, snacks and drinks. £

Burger King

Lower Concourse
The Peacocks
Woking
Surrey GU21 6GB
01483 728159
www.burgerking.co.uk

■ *Mon-Wed 09:00-18:00, Thu 09:00-20:00, Fri-Sat 09:00-18:00, Sun 10:00-17:00*
Fast food outlet serving burger style menu. Children's menu available with free toy. £

KFC

Lower Concourse
The Peacocks
Woking
Surrey GU21 6GB
01483 755954
www.kfc.co.uk

■ *Mon-Wed 10:30-18:00, Thu 10:30-20:00, Fri 10:30-18:00, Sat 10:00-18:00, Sun 11:00-17:00*
Fast food outlet serving southern fried chicken menu. Children's menu available. Will provide water to heat baby food. £

Le Papillon Patisserie

Lower Concourse
The Peacocks
Woking
Surrey GU21 6GB
01483 771244

■ *Mon-Fri 09:30-17:30, Sat 09:00-17:30, Sun 10:00-16.00*
French Patisserie/Boulangerie style café, serving cakes, sandwiches, salads and soups. Children's lunch boxes provided and smaller portions of adult options also available. Will heat baby food and milk on request. £

McDonald's

Lower Concourse
The Peacocks
Woking
Surrey GU21 1GQ
01483 726765
www.mcdonalds.co.uk

■ *Mon-Thu 07:00-23:00, Fri-Sat 07:00-00:00, Sun 07:00-23:00*
Fast food restaurant serving burger style menu. Smaller portion children's meals available with free toy.
£

Pizza Hut Express

Lower Concourse
The Peacocks
Woking
Surrey GU21 6GH
01483 762809

■ *Mon-Wed 10:00-18:00, Thu 10:00-20:00, Fri-Sat 10:00-18:00, Sun 11:00-17:00*
Fast food restaurant with a selection of pizzas. Also provides unlimited soft drinks and ice cream. £

Spud-U-Like

Lower Concourse
The Peacocks
Woking
Surrey GU21 6GB
01483 750326

www.spudulike.co.uk

■ *Mon-Fri 09:00-18:00, Sat-Sun 10:00-17:00*

Fast food outlet serving jacket potatoes with a wide range of fillings. Hot and cold drinks and a few cakes available. £

WOKING TOWN CENTRE

Most of the establishments in Woking Town centre do not have free parking so you need to park in one of the town centre car parks.

The Restaurant at Allders of Woking

Upper Concourse
The Peacocks
Woking
Surrey GU21 1GE
01483 732754

■ *Mon-Fri 09:30-17:00, Sat 09:00-17:00, Sun 10:30-16:30*

Department store restaurant serving hot and cold meals, snacks and drinks. Children's menu available. Heinz baby food sold. If adult meals are over £5 then child's meal is free. Will heat baby food and milk on request. 6 highchairs. £

The Beacon Coffee Shop

Christ Church
Town Square
Woking
Surrey GU21 6YG
01483 740897
www.ccwoking.org.uk

■ *Mon-Fri 10:00-14:00, Sat 10:30-13.30*

Counter service café serving meals, snacks and drinks with some outdoor seating. Will heat baby food and milk on request.Lego table available for children to play with. 2 highchairs. £

Big Apple Diner

Chertsey Road
Woking
Surrey GU21 1HR
01483 727100

■ *Mon-Sun 12:00-22:30*

Fast food diner at entertainment establishment which includes bowling, soft play and amusements. See entry 'House of Play' in Places to Go section. 5 highchairs. £

Burger King

Unit 27a
The Peacocks
Woking
Surrey GU21 6GB
01483 762128
www.burgerking.co.uk

■ *Mon-Sat 09:00-21:00, Sun 10:00-21:00*

Fast food outlet serving burger style menu. Children's menu available with free toy. 3 highchairs. £

Café Centrale

11 Church Path
Woking
Surrey GU21 1EG
01483 724532

■ *Mon-Sat 07:30-17:30, Sun 10:00-14:00*

Café with counter service serving Italian dishes and sweets. Children's menu includes pasta, nuggets, chips and sandwiches. Will heat baby food on request. 4 highchairs. £

Café Giardino

41 Wolsey Walk
Woking
Surrey GU21 6X5
www.giardinogroup.co.uk/restaurants.asp

■ *Mon-Sat 09:00-17:30, Sun 11:00-17:00*

Café selling wide range of hot and cold

food. 2 main meal options available in a smaller portion. 3 highchairs.
£

Esquires

53 Commercial Way
Woking
Surrey GU21 6HN
01483 727322
www.esquirescoffee.com

■ *Mon-Fri 07:30-19:00,*
Sat 08:30-18:00, Sun 10:30-17:00
Coffee house offering full range of coffee, tea and other beverages. Sandwiches, toasted paninis, cakes and fruit are available. Will microwave baby food and milk on request. 3 highchairs. £

Hugo's Bar & Brasserie

Church Street East
Woking
Surrey GU21 1HA
01483 221111
www.holiday-inn.com/wokinguk

■ *Mon-Thu 12:30-15:00, 17:30-22:00,*
Fri 12:30-15:00, 17:30-23:00,
Sat 17:30-23:00, Sun 20:30-21.30.
Bar open for light snacks at weekend.
Hotel restaurant serving freshly cooked, international cuisine. Weekends are better for families, as the hotel is more business orientated during the week. Children's menu and crayons provided. Special dietary needs are accommodated. Will heat baby food and milk on request. Non smoking area. 5 highchairs.
££

Jaipur

49 Chertsey Road
Woking
Surrey GU21 5AJ
01483 772626
www.jaipurrestaurant.co.uk
info@jaipurrestaurant.co.uk

■ *Mon-Sun 12:00-14:30, 18:00-23:30*
Indian restaurant that has won awards for food. Family buffet with choice of 10 dishes every Sunday 12:30-14:30, during which children under 8 eat for free. Limited to one child per adult. Will heat baby food on request. Plenty of space for pushchairs. Non smoking area. 1 highchair. **££**

KFC

29-31 Chertsey Road
Woking
Surrey GU21 5AJ
01483 740777
www.kfc.co.uk

■ *Mon-Wed 11:00-00:00,*
Thu-Fri 11:00-03:00, Sat 10:30-03:00
Southern fried chicken fast food outlet with eat in and takeaway. Children's menu and eating area. 2 highchairs.
£

McDonald's

11-17 Chertsey Road
Woking
Surrey GU21 5AB
01483 729755

■ *Mon-Thu 07:00-23:00,*
Fri-Sat 07:00-00:00, Sun 07:00-23:00
Fast food restaurant serving burger style menu. Smaller portion children's meals available with free toy. Balloons upstairs. Highchairs available.
£

Muffin Break

Unit 3, Bandstand Mall
The Peacocks
Woking
Surrey GU21 1GB
01483 773554
www.muffinbreak.co.uk

■ *Mon-Sat 09:00-18:00,*
Sun 10:00-17:00
Café selling freshly baked savoury and sweet muffins, a range of hot and cold

drinks and cakes. Children's options available. 2 highchairs. £

Peter's Palace
48 Chertsey Road
Woking
Surrey GU21 5PG
01483 770605

■ *Mon-Sun 12:00-16:00, 18:00-23:30*
Chinese restaurant. Children's menu. Will warm baby food and milk on request. 2 highchairs. ££

Pizza Express
65-67 Goldsworth Road
Woking
Surrey GU21 1LJ
01483 750310
www.pizzaexpress.com

■ *Mon-Sat 12:00-23:30, Sun 12:00-23:00*
Restaurant serving pizza, pasta, salads and puddings. Non smoking area. 6 highchairs. ££ P

Pizza Hut
19-21 Chertsey Road
Woking
Surrey GU21 5AB
01483 755845
www.pizzahut.co.uk

■ *Mon-Thu 11:30-22:00,*
Fri-Sat 11:30-23:00, Sun 12:00-22:00
Restaurant serving pizza, pasta, salad and puddings. Children's menu includes pizza, chicken or pasta. Unlimited ice cream factory with choice of toppings. Free goodie bags provided with Kid's meal. Will provide hot water to warm milk and baby food. No smoking throughout. 5 highchairs. £

Subway
9 Chertsey Road
Woking
Surrey GU21 5AB
01483 599191

■ *Mon-Thu 10:00-22:30,*
Fri-Sat 10:00-03:00, Sun 10:00-00:00
Sandwich shop with seating. Children's menu includes toy, drink and sandwich. Healthy eating/vegetarian options available. Provide deli bread with no seeds or nuts in for children. Will provide hot water to warm baby food and milk. 2 highchairs. £

J.D.Wetherspoon
51-59 Chertsey Road
Woking
Surrey GU21 5AJ
01483 722818
www.jdwetherspoon.co.uk

■ *Sun 12:00-16:00 children welcome if eating with parents*
Pub with no smoking eating area. Children's menu includes pizza, spaghetti bolognese and burgers. Will heat baby food on request. Children given colouring book and crayons. Highchairs available. ££ . P

OUT OF TOWN

Bird in Hand Restaurant
Egley Road
Mayford
Surrey GU22 0NL
01483 756320

■ *Tue 18:30-22:00,*
Wed-Sun 12:00-14:30, 18:30-22:00
Italian and English restaurant with garden. No specific children's menu but will provide smaller portions. Pub next door converting to buffet style restaurant in near future. Restaurant is non smoking. 2 highchairs.
£££ . P

The Bridge Barn
Bridge Barn Lane
Horsell
Woking
Surrey GU21 1NL
01483 763642/08701 977276

www.eatingoutandout.co.uk

■ *Mon-Thu 12:00-14:30, 18:00-22:00, Fri 12:00-14:30, 18:00-22:30 Sat 12:00-22:30, Sun 12:00-21:00*

Stylish pub restaurant offering range of modern and traditional dishes. Separate pub snack menu, also a cheaper daytime menu. Separate children's menus for under 7's and 7-12 years with healthy eating options. Jars of baby food provided. Will also heat milk and baby food on request. Wheelchair/double buggy access into the building but not upstairs into the restaurant. Non smoking area. 10 highchairs. **££** **P**

Blubeckers White Hart

High Street
Chobham
Surrey GU24 8AA
01276 857580
www.blubeckers.co.uk

■ *Mon-Thu 12:00-14:30, 17:30-22:00, Fri 12:00-15:00, 17:30-22:30, Sat 12:00-15:00, 17:30-22:30, Sun 12:00-16:00, 17:30-21:30*

Restaurant serving range of meals. Large children's menu includes pasta, chicken, spaghetti bolognese and salad. Will warm baby food and milk on request and can breastfeed in privacy in office. Non smoking area. 10 highchairs and 2 booster seats.
££ **P**

Café Braggs

Talbot Hotel
High Street
Ripley
Surrey GU23 6BD
01483 225188

■ *Mon-Sun 12:30-14:30, 18:30-21:30*

Café is part of main hotel. Children's menu includes spaghetti bolognese and chicken nuggets. Smoking throughout. 3 highchairs. **££** **P**

Castle Grove

Castle Grove Road
Chobham
Surrey GU24 8EE
01276 858196

■ *Mon-Thu 11:00-14:30, 17:30-23:00, Fri 11:00-15:00, 17:30-23:00, Sat 11:00-15:30, 18:00-23:00, Sun 12:00-15:00, 19:00-22:30*

Real pub with fenced garden which has swings, slides and bouncy castle. Children's menu. Children welcome in bar area if eating with adult. Pub is smoking throughout. **££** **P**

Cricketers Inn

Horsell Birch
Woking
Surrey GU21 4XB
01483 762363

■ *Mon-Fri 12:00-14:30, 18:00-21:30, Sat-Sun 11:00-23:00 (restaurant opening times)*

Traditional old-fashioned pub with 60 seater restaurant. Children's menu with healthy eating/vegetarian options. Will warm baby food or milk on request. Play area outside with bouncy castle some Saturdays and Bank Holidays. Can breastfeed in baby changing area. Colouring pencils available. Non smoking area. 3 highchairs and 5 booster seats.
££ **P**

Crown and Anchor-Chippy's Thai Experience

100 High Street
Old Woking
Surrey GU22 9LN
01483 766274

■ *Mon-Fri 12:00-14:00, 18:00-22:00, Sat 18:00-22:00, Sun 12:00-21:00*

Thai restaurant completely separate from pub area. Also serving some English food such as Sunday roast. Garden with picnic benches. Children's menu. Will warm baby food and milk on request. Access for pushchairs but limited space inside. Pub and restaurant are smoking. Highchairs available on request (need to ask before you go to restaurant). **££** **P**

Emma Hamiltons

Talbot Hotel
High Street
Ripley
Surrey GU23 6BB
01483 225188
www.talbothotel.net
enquiries@talbothotel.net

■ *Mon-Sun 12:00-14:30, 18:30-21:30*

Restaurant (pub and small hotel also on site) that was originally an old coaching inn. Children's menu. Will happily accommodate special dietary requirements. Will find you a quiet room to breastfeed in. Enclosed garden that is safe for children to play in. Smoking throughout. Highchairs available. **£££** **P**

Fox Inn

333 Guildford Road
Bisley
Woking
Surrey GU24 9AB
01483 473175

■ *Mon-Sat 11:00-23:00,*
Sun 12:00-22:30

Pub with separate restaurant and garden. Children's menu. Happy to accommodate special dietary requirements. Will heat baby food and milk on request. Children welcome in pub up to 19:30, or later if dining with adults in restaurant. Pushchairs encouraged to be collapsed inside. Smoking throughout. 2 highchairs.
££ **P**

Hautboy Inn

Ockham Lane
Ockham
Surrey GU23 6NP
01483 225355
thehautboy@aol.com

■ *Mon-Sat 12:00-14:30, 19:00-21:30,*
Sun 12:00-16:00

Five bedroom hotel with pub and restaurant. Children's menu. Will warm baby food and milk on request. Restaurant has 2 small steps (pub is upstairs) but can lift pushchair over. Restaurant is non smoking. 2 highchairs. **££** **P**

Hungry Horse

The King's Arms
42 High Street
Bagshot
Surrey GU19 5AZ
01276 473812
www.hungryhorse.co.uk

■ *Mon-Sat 11:30-23:00,*
Sun 12:00-22:30

Pub restaurant serving wide range of food on a 17" plate! Large choice children's menu including healthy eating options. Pick'n'mix deal for kids includes burgers, pizza, jacket potato and salad. Will heat baby food and milk on request. Colouring materials available. No bookings taken. Restaurant is non smoking. 6 highchairs. **££** **P**

Jovial Sailor

Portsmouth Road
Ripley
Surrey GU23 6EZ
01483 224360

■ *Mon-Sun 11:00-23:00*

Traditional British pub with separate non-smoking area. Has won Guildford Pub of Year 2003. Children's menu. Will warm baby food and milk on request. Lots of quiet corners if you want to breastfeed. Non smoking area. 2 highchairs. **££**

King's House Coffee Shop

14 High Street
Knaphill
Woking
Surrey GU21 2PE
01483 799758
www.kings-house.co.uk

■ *Mon-Fri 09:30-15:00, Sat 10:00-14:30*

Coffee shop serving wide range of snacks and hot dishes including a roast dinner every Wednesday. Children's menu available with healthy options. Will heat baby food and milk on request. Toys for children to play with. 2 highchairs and 2 booster seats.
£ P **£**

Little Chef

A3 Ripley Bypass
Ripley
Surrey GU23 6PT
01483 225115 (northbound), 01483 225138 (southbound)
www.little-chef.co.uk

■ *Mon-Sun 07:00-22:00*

Service station restaurant. Very cheap children's menu with healthy eating options. Free baby food. Will heat baby food and milk on request. Free drinks refills. 4 highchairs.
££ P

Mayford Arms

Guildford Road
Mayford
Woking
Surrey GU22 9PT
01483 761018

■ *Mon-Sat 11:00-23:00, Sun 12:00-22:30 (Children welcome until 21:30)*

Family pub that serves food. Children's menu. Enclosed garden with swing. Non-smoking restaurant area.
££ P

Mogul

142 Connaught Road
Brookwood
Surrey GU24 0AS
01483 472610

■ *Tue –Sun 17:30-23:30 open Bank Holidays but then closed Tue*

Indian restaurant. Will accomodate children's dietary requirements. Smoking throughout. 1 highchair.
££ P

Otter Harvester

Guildford Road
Ottershaw
Surrey KT16 0PQ
01932 873217

■ *Mon-Sun 12:00-22:00*

Pub with family restaurant and large garden. Early Bird offers with 1/3 off meals Mon-Fri from 12:00-18:30, Sat-Sun 12:00-17:00. Have specific children's menu for under 5's and over 5's. Will open and warm baby food that is in a sealed jar. Children welcome in side room of pub and in restaurant. Children's cutlery on request. Non smoking area. 9 highchairs. **££** P

Parkway (Brewers Fayre)

Stoke Road
Guildford
Surrey GU1 1UP
08701 977122
www.brewersfayre.co.uk

■ *Mon-Sat 11:30-22:00, Sun 12:00-22:00*

Pub restaurant with a patio area. Children's menu available with healthy eating options. Will only open and warm baby food in a sealed jar. Jars of baby food available at a small charge. Colouring sheets and pencils provided. No bookings taken. Non smoking area.4 highchairs.
££ P

Plough Inn
Cheapside
Horsell
Woking
Surrey GU21 4JL
01483 714105

■ *Mon-Sat 11:00-23:00, Sun 12:00-22:30*
Pub with enclosed garden that includes slide and sandpit. Children's menu. Smoking throughout. 2 highchairs. **££**

Princess
Princess Road
Maybury
Woking
Surrey GU22 8EQ
01483 726879

■ *Mon-Fri 12:00-14:00, 18:00-20:00, Sat 12:00-20:00, Sun 12:00-18:00 (opening times for food)*
Children are welcome up until 21:00
Pub with family room and enclosed garden. Children's menu. Play area and indoor and outdoor toys. Smoking throughout. **££**

Red Lion Pub
Red Lion Road
Chobham
Surrey GU24 8RG
01276 858813

■ *Mon-Sat 11:00-23:00, Sun 12:00-22:30*
Pub with separate large dining area and bed and breakfast. Children's menu. Will warm up baby food and milk on request. Garden with play area and sometimes has a bouncy castle. Restaurant is non smoking. 1 highchair. **££**

The Rowbarge
39 St.John's Road
St.John's
Woking
Surrey GU21 1SA
01483 761618

■ *Mon-Fri 11:00-15:00, 17:00-23:00, Sat-Sun 11:00-23:00*
Pub restaurant with large garden. Children's menu. Will warm baby food and milk on request. Non smoking area. 2 highchairs and booster seats.
££

St Andrew's Coffee Shop
Goldsworth Park Centre
Woking
Surrey GU21 3LG
01483 723879
standrews@goldsworthpark.org.uk

■ *Tue-Fri 10:00-14:00*
Coffee shop serving a variety of coffees, toasted sandwiches, home made soup, jacket potatoes and salads. Children's lunch pack available. Will heat baby food and milk on request. Separate room with tables and seating for adults and play equipment for children. 4 highchairs.
£

Sunrise Café at Squires Garden Centre
Littlewick Road
Chobham
Woking
Surrey GU21 4XR
01276 858978

■ *Mon-Sat 09:00-17:00, Sun 10:00-16:30*
Café with waitress service, serving drinks, light meals and snacks. Children's menu. Will heat baby food and milk on request. 2 highchairs.
£

Superfish
51 Old Woking Road
West Byfleet
Surrey KT14 6LG
01932 340366

■ *Mon-Fri 11:30-14:00, 17:00-22:30,*

Sat 11:30-14:00, 17:00-23:00
Fish and chip restaurant. Children's menu includes smaller portions of fish and chicken nuggets. Will warm baby food and milk on request. Parking is pay on road. 2 highchairs. **££**

Surrey Homespread

Hermitage Road
St. John's
Woking
Surrey GU21 1TX
01483 474312

■ *Mon-Sat 11:00-23:00, Sun 12:00-22:30*
Pub restaurant. Children's menu includes vegetarian/healthy eating options. Will provide hot water to warm baby food and milk. Quieter areas if want to breastfeed. Soft play area indoors. Provide children's parties. Non smoking area. 6 highchairs. **££ P**

The White Hart

White Hart Lane
Wood Street Village
Worplesdon
Surrey GU3 5DX
01483 235939

■ *Mon-Thu 11:30-15:00, 18:30-21:00, Fri-Sat 11:30-21:30, Sun 11:30-20:30 (children's licensing hours)*
Pub with restaurant. Garden with picnic benches. Children's menu includes healthy eating options and refillable fizzy drink. Will warm baby food on request and has private area if want to breastfeed. Children can stay in restaurant until closing time (23:00) if they have eaten. Restaurant is non smoking.
££ P

Windle Brook (Brewer's Fayre)

39 London Road
Bagshot
Surrey GU19 5HR
01276 479942
www.brewersfayre.co.uk

■ *Mon-Sat 11:00-23:00, Sun 12:00-22:30*
Pub restaurant with enclosed patio area. Children's menu with healthy eating options. Will only open and warm baby food in a sealed jar. Colouring sheets and pencils provided. Non smoking area.10 highchairs.
££ P

Worplesdon Place - Out and Out

Perry Hill
Worplesdon
Surrey GU3 3RY
01483 232407
www.eatingoutandout.co.uk

■ *Mon-Sun 11:00-23:00*
Restaurant with separate bar and large garden with play area. Children's menu for over 5's and under 5's including healthy eating options. Will accommodate dietary requirements on request. Free jar of baby food. Will warm baby food on request. Children welcome in bar area and restaurant. Restaurant is non smoking. Highchairs available. **££ P**

Yeoman Harvester

81 Old Woking Road
West Byfleet
Surrey KT14 6JA
01932 344553

■ *Mon-Sun 12:00-22:00*
Pub with family restaurant. Early Bird offers with 1/3 off meals Mon-Fri from 12:00-18:30, Sat-Sun 12:00-17:00. Have specific children's menu for under 5's and over 5's with healthy eating options. Will provide hot water to warm baby food and milk. Non smoking area. 8 highchairs.
££ P

Zinfandel
1 Bagshot Road
Chobham
Surrey GU24 8BP
01276 858491

■ *Mon-Sat 12:00-15:00, 18:00-22:00, Sun 12:00-16:00, 18:00-22:00*
Modern restaurant serving Napa Valley cuisine such as steak, salad, pizza and seafood. Children's menu includes ice cream, soft drink and choice of pasta, pizza or chicken. Will heat baby food on request. Branches also in Guildford and Weybridge. Non smoking area.
5 highchairs. **£££**

Shopping

SHOPPING IS a very different experience once you've had a child. Babies need changing facilities and possibly somewhere that you can feed them whilst older ones need toilet facilities and constant stimulation. It helps tremendously if you know exactly where to go for what you want and we have included sections on most of the things you are likely to want to buy such as clothes, shoes, toys and equipment. Knowing in advance that the shop or supermarket you are going to has baby changing facilities or toilets nearby can make the trip much easier so we have included a list of facilities available in Woking.

BOOKS

Corbetts

12 Station approach
West Byfleet
Surrey KT14 6NG
01932 344269

■ *Mon-Sat 09:00-17:00*

General bookstore with children's section including reading area with toys/book characters. Parking in nearby pay and display car park.

Ottakars

Upper Concourse
Peacocks Centre
Woking
Surrey GU21 1GD
01483 767564
woking@ottakars.co.uk

■ *Mon-Wed 09:30-18:00, Thu 09:30-20:00, Fri 09;30-18:00, Sat 09:00-18:00, Sun 11:00-17:00*

General bookstore with large children's section and rocking horse. Email and phone orders taken.

Ottakars

18 Wolsey Walk
Woking
Surrey GU21 1XU
01483 763322
wokingwolsey@ottakars.co.uk

■ *Mon-Sat 09:00-17:30, Sun 11:00-17:00*

General bookstore with children's section including play/activity table. Email and phone orders taken.

RHS Garden Wisley

Wisley
Surrey GU23 6QB
01483 211113
www.rhs.org.uk

■ *Mon-Sat 10:00-17:30, Sun 11:00-17:00*

Shop with wide range of children's books and some children's gifts. P

WH Smith

41-43 Commercial Way
Woking
Surrey GU21 6XR
01483 770603
www.whsmith.co.uk

■ *Mon-Sat 08:45-17:30, Sun 11:00-17:00*

General bookstore with some children's books. Videos and DVDs also stocked. Online ordering available.

CLOTHES

Adams Childrenswear

8-10 Wolsey Walk
Wolsey Walk
Woking
Surrey GU21 6XU
01483 724228
www.adams.co.uk

■ *Mon-Sat 09:30-17:30, Sun 11:00-16:30*

Wide variety of children's clothing from babies upwards.

Bambini

27 Church Street
Weybridge
Surrey KT13 8DF
01932 857665

■ *Mon-Sat 09:30-17:00*

Clothing from newborn-10yrs. Toys also stocked. P

B Wise

Premier House
Market Square
Woking
Surrey GU21 1DG

01483 770877

■ *Mon-Sat 09:00-17:30, Sun 11:00-17:00*
A range of children's clothing available.

Baby Gap/Gap Kids

68 High Street
Guildford
Surrey GU1 3ES
01483 302959
www.gapkids.com
www.babygap.com

■ *Mon-Sat 09:00-18:00, Sun 11:00-17:00*
Clothing from newborn-13yrs. No access for double buggy to Baby Gap on top floor as lift is too small.

BHS

81 Commercial Way
Woking
Surrey GU21 1HN
01483 722727
www.bhs.com

■ *Mon-Thu 09:00-17:30, Fri-Sat 09:00-18:00, Sun 11:00-17:00*
Range of children's clothing available.

Kidz Bitz

14-16 Alexandra Road
North Camp
Farnborough
Hampshire GU14 6DA
01252 544263

■ *Tue, Thu-Fri 10:00-17:00*
Stocks a range of new and used quality clothes for children from newborn-5 yrs. Will also pay cash for all Next, Gap and M&S items in excellent condition and other quality children's clothing. Small range of christening wear and toys. **P**

Kids Kaper

01483 772443
07941 952094 (Mobile)
www.kidskaper.co.uk
enquiries@kidskaper.co.uk

Swimwear, sunsuits, baby shoes, outdoor wear, girls wear. Ranges such as Boboli and Babu. Some boys wear available. Also buggy snuggles, cosy toes and blankets. Home delivery service and online ordering only.

Little Rumours

130 Oatlands Drive
Weybridge
Surrey KT13 9HL
01932 854416

■ *Mon 10:00-17:30, Tue-Sat 09:30-17:30*
Clothing from newborn-18mths including Baby Clair, Mini and Tuff stocked. **P**

Marks and Spencer

Barns Wallis Drive
Weybridge
Surrey KT13 0XF
01932 256345
www.marksandspencer.com

■ *Mon-Fri 09:00-22:00, Sat 08:30-22:00, Sun 10:00-16:00*
Wide range of clothing from newborn-4 yrs. Restaurant. Mail order catalogue and online ordering available.
P

Marks and Spencer

61 Guildford High Street
Guildford
Surrey GU1 3EB
01483 502420
www.marksandspencer.com

■ *Mon-Wed 09:00-18:00, Thu 09:00-20:00, Fri-Sat 08:30-18:30, Sun 11:00-17:00*
Children's clothes, babywear and schoolwear. Some toys stocked. Café

on top floor. Mail order catalogue and online ordering available.

Marks and Spencer

The Meadows
Marshall Road
Sandhurst
Berkshire GU47 0FD
01276 31031
www.marksandspencer.com

■ *Mon-Fri 09:00-22:00, Sat 08:00-22:00, Sun 11:00-17:00*

One of largest stores with an extensive range of clothing from newborn to adult. Schoolwear, homeware including nursery ranges. Children's toys, books and videos. Mail order catalogue and online ordering available. Parent and child parking.

Monsoon

Unit 56-57 Peacocks Centre
Woking
Surrey GU21 1GD
01483 740287
www.monsoon.co.uk

■ *Mon-Wed 09:00-18:00, Thu 09:30-20:00, Sat 09:00-18:00, Sun 11:00-17:00*

Baby wear and children's clothes, boys from newborn-8yrs and girls from newborn-12yrs. Home delivery service available.

Narnia

97 Queens Road
Weybridge
Surrey KT13 9UQ
www.narniaofweybridge.co.uk

■ *Mon-Fri 09:30-17:30, Sat 10:00-17:30*

Designer childrenswear from newborn

to 8yrs. Home delivery service on request, online ordering available. A few toys available to keep little ones occupied.

Next

Middle Concourse
The Peacocks
Woking
Surrey GU21 1GD
01483 741450
www.next.co.uk

■ *Mon-Wed 09:30-18:00, Thu 09:30-20:00, Fri-Sat 09:00-18:00, Sun 11:00-17:00*

Clothing from newborn-10yrs. Mail order catalogue and online ordering available for clothing from newborn-16yrs.

T K Maxx

Lower Concourse
The Peacocks
Woking
Surrey GU21 1GA
01483 771660
www.tkmaxx.com

■ *Mon-Wed 09:30-18:00, Thu 09:30-20:00, Fri 09:30-18:00, Sat 09:00-18:00, Sun 11:00-17:00*

Clothes and toys from newborn-16yrs.

DANCE, SPORT AND SPECIAL OCCASION WEAR

Cabaret Dancewear

3 Cresswell Corner
Anchor Hill
Knaphill
Woking
Surrey GU21 2JD
01483 488440

■ *Mon-Fri 10:00-17:30, Sat 10:00-17:00*

Wide selection of dancewear including RAD and ISTD uniforms, costumes, fancy dress, skate dresses and accessories. Bridesmaid shoes and communion dresses. Ballet, tap, pointe, jazz and ballroom shoes. From 2yrs upwards. Can phone and order, and shop will deliver to you.

Charlotte's Dancewear

86 High Road
Byfleet
Surrey KT14 7QW
01932 340958

■ *Mon-Fri 09:00-17:30, Sat 09:00-17:00*

Wide selection of dancewear including RAD and ISTD uniform. Local dance school uniforms, skating dresses, gym outfits, hair accessories. Ballet, pointe, tap, jazz and ballroom shoes. Bridesmaid and pageboy shoes. Brownie, Guide, Cub and Scout uniforms. From 2yrs upwards.

Dancer's World and Swimscene

18 London Road
Blackwater
Surrey GU17 9AA
01276 600935

■ *Mon-Fri 10:00-17:30, Sat 09:30-17:00*

Wide selection of dancewear including RAD and ISTD uniforms. Ballet, pointe, tap, jazz and ballroom shoes. Gymwear, skating wear, swimwear and equipment. From babies upwards.

Flashdance

44 Alexandra Road
North Camp
Farnborough
Hampshire GU14 6DA
01252 512612

■ *Tue-Sat 09:30-17:00*

Wide selection of dancewear including RAD and ISTD uniforms. Ballet, tap, jazz, ballroom and pointe shoes. Gymnastics, skater and majorette outfits. Large selection of professional make-up, dance accessories and bridal shoes. From 2yrs upwards.

Griffiths and Schoolgirl by Valentino

23-27 The Broadway
Knaphill
Woking
Surrey GU21 2DR
01483 473357

■ *Mon-Sat 09:00-17:30*
Wide selection of dancewear including RAD and ISTD uniforms. Ballet, jazz and tap shoes. Brownie, Guide, Cub and Scout uniforms, school uniforms, and childrenswear. From babies upwards.

Howzat School and Leisure Services

210 London Road
Burpham
Guildford
Surrey GU4 7JS
01483 577835
www.howzatonline.co.uk

■ *Mon-Sat 09:00-17:30*
Sports equipment, clothing and schoolwear from 4yrs upwards. Online ordering available.

Janet's Dancewear and School Uniform

82 St Jude Road
Englefield Green
Egham
Surrey TW20 0DF
01784 436301

■ *Mon-Fri 09:30-17:30, Sat 10:00-17:00, school holidays and half terms 10:00-17:00*
Wide selection of dancewear including RAD and ISTD uniforms, local dance school uniforms, dance costumes, school uniforms and fancy dress. Ballet, tap, jazz, ballroom and pointe shoes. Brownie, Guide, Beaver, Cub and Scout uniforms. Selection of baby wear. Newborn to adult.

SHOES

Clarks Shoes

Mothercare World
The Paddock Retail Park
Sopwith Way
Brooklands
Weybridge
Surrey KT13 0XF
01932 342037

■ *Mon-Fri 09:00-19:00, Sat 09:00-18:00, Sun 10:00-16:00*
Shop within Mothercare World, selling a wide range of shoes from size 3 upwards. Bead table.

Clarks Shoes

The Peacocks
Unit 13-14 (Middle Concourse)
Woking
Surrey GU21 1GB
01483 761597
08705 134830 (Helpline)

■ *Mon-Wed 09:30-18:00, Thu 09:30-20:00, Fri 09:00-18:00, Sun 11:00-17:00*
Shoes from size 3 upwards, variety of styles and fittings. Bead table.

Start-rite at Instep
3-4 Chapel Street
Woking
Surrey GU21 1BY
01483 730634

■ *Mon-Sat 09:00-17:30, Sun 11:00-17:00*
Stock wide range of styles and fittings from size 2 upwards with a choice of 6 width fittings. Books to keep little ones entertained.

SUPERMARKETS

Sainsburys
Redding Way
Knaphill
Woking
Surrey GU21 2QT
01483 799601
www.sainsburys.co.uk

■ *Mon-Fri 07:00-23:00, Sat 07:00-22:00, Sun 10:00-16:00*
Café, approx 30 parent and child parking spaces. Adams clothing and Early Learning Centre toys available in store. Online ordering and delivery available. P

Safeway
82 Goldsworth Road
Woking
Surrey GU21 6LJ
01483 755552
www.safeway.com

■ *Mon-Sat 08:00-22:00, Sun 10:00-16:00*
Restaurant/café, 27 parent and child car park spaces. P

Tesco
Barnes Wallis Drive
Brooklands
Weybridge

Surrey KT13 0XF
01932 747400
www.tesco.com

■ *Open 24hrs Mon 08:00-Sat 22:00, Sun 10:00-16:00*
Upstairs café with large lift, 26 parent and child parking spaces. Online ordering and delivery available.
P

Tesco

The Meadows
Marshall Road
Sandhurst
Surrey GU47 0FD
www.tesco.com

■ *Open 24hrs Mon 08:00-Sat 22:00, Sun 10:00-16:00*
Upstairs café with large lift. Parent and child parking spaces. Large range of children's clothing and toys from newborn-16yrs. On line ordering and delivery available.
P

Waitrose

60 Station Approach
West Byfleet
Surrey KT14 6NE
01932 351028
www.waitrose.com

■ *Mon-Tue 08:30-19:00, Wed-Thu 08:30-20:00, Fri 08:30-21:00, Sat 08:30-19:00, Sun 10:00-16:00*
5 parent & child spaces.
P

Waitrose

1 Goldsworth Park Centre
Denton Way
Woking
Surrey GU21 3LG
01483 725574
www.waitrose.com

■ *Mon-Tue 08:30-19:00, Wed-Thu 08:30-20:00, Fri 08:30-21:00, Sat 08:30-19:00, Sun 10:00-16:00*
6 parent and child spaces. P

TOYS AND EQUIPMENT

Allders

The Peacocks
Woking
Surrey GU21 1GE
01483 766488

■ *Mon-Wed 09:30-18:00, Thu 09:30-20:00, Fri 09:30-18:00, Sat 09:00-18:00, Sun 11:00-17:00*
Babies and children's clothing, and range of toys stocked. Home delivery available.

Argos

34 Commercial Way
Woking
Surrey GU21 1EN
01483 720528

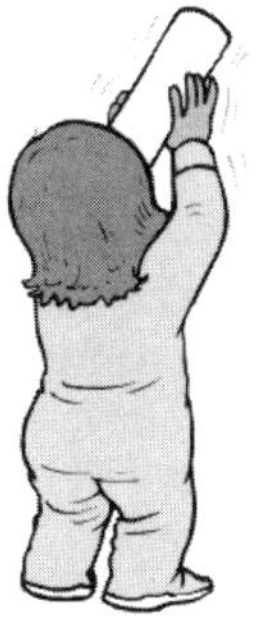

www.argos.co.uk

■ *Mon-Sat 09:00-17:30, Sun 11:00-16:00*
Toys and baby equipment from new-born upwards stocked. Mail order catalogue and online ordering available.

Baby Bargains of Ash

59 Guildford Road
Ash
Surrey GU12 6BQ
01252 326916

■ *Tue-Thu 10:00-16:00, Sat 10:00-16:00*
Nearly new clothes, nursery equipment, high chairs and toys. New equipment such as pushchairs and bedding. Local home delivery service.

Babygear

1 Portsebery Road
Camberley
Surrey GU15 3SZ
01276 20404

■ *Mon-Sat 09:00-17:30*
Nursery equipment, pushchairs, cots, highchairs and small range of toys. From newborn-4yrs. Local home delivery free within 10 mile radius. Mail order service available.
P

The Baby's Room

11 Tunsgate
Guildford
Surrey GU1 3QT
01483 300806

■ *Mon-Fri 10:35-17:00, Sat 09:45-17:30*
A wide variety of children's clothes, toys and equipment sold. Local home delivery available.

Boots

1-9 Commercial Way
Woking
Surrey GU21 1YA
01483 761648

■ *Mon-Tue 08:35-17:45, Wed 09:00-17:45, Thu-Sat 08:35-17:45, Sun 11:00-17:00*
Children's clothing and shoes from newborn-4yrs. Selection of toys stocked.Baby equipment such as bottles, sterilizers and baby food.

Daisy and Tom

12a North Street
Guildford
Surrey GU1 4AF
01483 207500
www.daisyandtom.com

■ *Mon-Sat 09:30-18:00, Sun 11:00-17:00*
Quality toys, book department,

pushchairs, nursery equipment, designer children's clothing and shoes. Home delivery service, online ordering and mail order available.

Early Learning Centre

19 Commercial Way
Woking
Surrey GU21 1XQ
01483 755751
www.elc.co.uk

■ *Mon-Sat 09:00-17:30, Sun 10:00-16:00*

Wide range of toys, games, books and dressing up clothes. Tuesday activity mornings where children can play with toys. Mail order catalogue and on ine ordering available.

Essentials

5 High Street
Weybridge
Surrey KT13 8AX
01932 858666

■ *Mon-Sat 09:30-17:30*

First gift items, wooden toys, educational toys and games. Items from newborn-7yrs. Large items delivered locally. Brio train layout to keep little ones occupied.

Funtasia

3 Oakdene Parade
Cobham
Surrey KT11 2LR
01932 867374

■ *Mon-Sat 09:30-17:30*

Wide variety of toys stocked. On line ordering available. P

Halfords Ltd

Lyon Retail Park
Oriental Road
Woking
Surrey GU22 8BD
01483 727550
www.halfords.com

■ *Mon-Fri 09:00-20:00, Sat 09:00-18:00, Sun 10:00-17:00*

Car seats and bikes sold. Online ordering available. P

Ikea Brent Park

2 Drury Way
North Circular Road
London
NW10 0TH
0845 355 1141
www.ikea.co.uk

■ *Mon-Fri 10:00-22:00, Sat 09:00-22:00, Sun 11:00-17:00*

Home furnishing including baby/child items such as toys and beds. Home delivery service. Ball park which closes 1/2 hour before store, where you can leave children aged 3-7yrs for 1hr. Restaurant has children's menu. Baby food/milk can be warmed on request. Will provide wheelchairs if needed.

P

Ikea Croydon

Valley Park
Purley Way
Croydon
Surrey CR0 4UZ
0845 355 1144
www.ikea.co.uk

■ *Mon-Fri 10:00-22:00, Sat 09:00-22:00, Sun 11:00-17:00*

Home furnishing including baby/child items such as toys and beds. Home delivery service. Ball park which closes 1/2 hr before store, where you can leave children aged 3-7yrs for 1hr. Restaurant has children's menu. Baby food/milk can be warmed on request.

P

Little B's The Baby Shop

7 Holly Parade
High Street
Cobham
Surrey KT11 3EE
01932 868294
www.thebabyshop.net
box@thebabyshop.net

■ *Mon-Sat 09:30-17:30*
Stock everything for the nursery plus clothing from newborn-6yrs. Online ordering and free delivery within 5-7 mile radius. Play table to keep little ones occupied.

Little Rascals

129 Princess Road
Maybury
Woking
Surrey GU22 8ER
01483 750555

■ *Tue-Fri 10:00-16:00, Sat 10:00-16:30*
Second hand clothes, shoes, toys, books and equipment sold.

Little Shop For Horrors

108b High Road
Byfleet
Surrey KT14 7QT
01932 341119

■ *Mon-Sat 10:00-16:00*
Second hand clothing from newborn-10yrs, buggies, nursery equipment, bedding, cots, travel cots, toys, safety equipment, baths, bouncers and walkers. Customers may bring goods, agree price and leave for 4 weeks - shop takes 50% of sale price when item is sold. Car park opposite. Will deliver goods by arrangement.

Longacres Garden Centre
London Road
Bagshot
Surrey GU19 5JB
01276 476778
www.longacres.co.uk
■ *Mon-Sat 08:30-17:00, Sun 10:30-16:30*
Some outdoor clothing, toys and garden toys stocked. Stockists for wooden play equipment. Small coffee shop.

Mothercare World
The Paddock Retail Park
Brooklands
Weybridge
Surrey KT13 0XF
■ *Mon-Fri 09:00-19:00, Sat 09:00-18:00, Sun 10:00-16:00*
Wide range of baby equipment and clothes from newbown-5yrs.

New Generation Baby
7 High Street
Knaphill
Woking
Surrey GU21 2PG
01483 481625
■ *Tue-Sat 09:30-17:00*
Baby equipment from newborn upwards. Includes clothes, toys, bedding, highchairs, pushchairs and christening outfits.

Notcutts Garden Centre
Waterers Nurseries
London Road
Bagshot
Surrey GU19 5DG
01276 472288
www.notcutts.co.uk
bagshot@notcutts.co.uk
■ *Mon-Sat 09:00-18:00 (Thu 09:00-20:00 Apr-Dec), Sun 10:30-16:30*
Gift shop, book shop and pet centre. Café with highchairs and children's menu. Will warm baby food/milk on request.

The Outdoor Toy Company Ltd
Notcutts Garden Centre
Waterers Nurseries
London Road
Bagshot
Surrey GU19 5JB
01276 451535
info@outdoortoycompany.co.uk
■ *Mon-Sat 09:00-18:00, Sun 10:30-16:30*
Trampolines, swings, slides, go carts, play houses, wooden systems, pull along wagons, pedal car and planes stocked. Free delivery for some items. Mail order catalogue and online ordering available.

Pixies
5 The Broadway
New Haw
Surrey KT15 3ES
01932 349864
gillianshanahan@yahoo.co.uk
■ *Mon-Tue 09:30-14:30, Thu-Fri 09:30-14:30, Sat 09:30-17:00*
New and second hand equipment, second hand toys, buggies and buggy boards, high chairs, cots, moses baskets (always new mattresses). Hire service and easy payment plan over number of weeks. Can deliver locally. Will warm baby food/milk on request.

Rainbow Play Systems Ltd
Hillier Garden Centre
London Road
Windlesham
Surrey GU20 6LQ
01344 874662
www.rainbowplay.co.uk

sales@rainbowplay.co.uk

■ *Mon-Sat 10:00-17:00,*
Sun 10:00-16:00
Stock play houses, climbing frames and big play sets. All wooden equipment decay resistant, full installation service. Can customise design and offer guidance on choice of suitable surfacing.

Raleigh Cycle Centre
48-54 Goldsworth Road
Woking
Surrey GU21 6LE
01483 722592
www.raleigh.co.uk

■ *Mon-Tue 09:30-17:30, Thu-Sat 09:00-17:30, Sun 11:00-17:00 (open on Wed during school holidays)*
Trikes and bikes sold. Online ordering available from main website.

Squires Garden Centre
Holloway Hill
Chertsey
Surrey KT16 0AE
01932 563727
www.squiresgardencentres.co.uk

■ *Summer 09:00-18:00,*
Winter 09:45-17:30
Outdoor toys stocked, home delivery service available.

Surrey Cycles Ltd
75 Station Road
Addlestone
Surrey KT15 2AR
01932 820716

■ *Mon-Sat 09:00-18:00,*
Sun 10:00-16:00
Wide range of bikes, bells and helmets sold. Local area delivery available. Will warm baby food/milk on request.

Switchback Cycles
31 High Street
Knaphill
Woking
Surrey GU21 2PP
01483 481773
www.switchbackcycles.com
simon@switchbackcycles.com

■ *Mon-Sat 09:00-17:30*
Bikes and accessories sold. Repair service for bikes and 3 wheel buggies. Home delivery service available.

Toys'R'Us
Church Street West
Woking
Surrey GU21 1HD
01483 726449
www.toysrus.co.uk

■ *Mon-Fri 09:00-20:00,*
Sat 09:00-19:00, Sun 11:00-17:00
Indoor and outdoor toys and games for all ages. Range of bikes and prams. Babies'R'Us stocks everything for baby including milk, food, nappies, cots and toys. Home delivery service and online ordering available.

Village Cycles
Unit 115 Between Streets
Cobham
Surrey KT11 1AA
01932 865911

■ *Mon-Fri 09:00-18:00,*
Sat 09:00-17:00, Sun 10:00-16:00
Children's bikes from 2 yrs upwards, helmets and bike accessories sold. Free local delivery.

Woking Models
1 Central Buildings
Chobham Road
Woking
Surrey GU21 6JH

01483 763023
www.wokingmodels.co.uk
shop@wokingmodels.co.uk
■ *Mon-Sat 09:00-18:00, Sun 11:00-14:00*
Models for the young through to sophisticated radio control cars for older children. Aircraft, cars, boats, trains, tank models. Commissions as well as standard items. Home delivery service available and online ordering available via e-mail.

Woolworths
Middle Concourse
The Peacocks
Woking
Surrey GU21 1GA
01483 751534
www.woolworths.co.uk
■ *Mon-Wed 09:30-18:00, Thu 09:30-20:00, Fri 09:30-18:00, Sat 09:00-18:00, Sun 11:00-17:00*
Ladybird clothing range from newborn upwards, shoes and toys stocked. Online ordering available.

Wyevale Garden Centre
New Haw Road
Addlestone
Weybridge
Surrey KT15 2BU
01932 845084
www.wyevale.co.uk
■ *Mon-Sat 09:00-18:00, Sun 10:30-16:00*
Toys, books, DVDs, garden furniture, videos and outdoor toys such as paddling pools sold. Restaurant with highchairs and children's menu. Home delivery service.

P

Wyevale Garden Centre
Egley Road
Woking
Surrey GU22 0NH
01483 714861
www.wyevale.co.uk
■ *Mon-Sat 09:00-18:00, Sun 10:30-16:00*
Wellingtons, hats, cards, books, fleeces and outdoor toys stocked. Self service coffee shop with highchairs. Home delivery service.

P

TOILET, CHANGING AND FEEDING FACILITIES

Allders Upper Concourse
The Peacocks Centre
Woking
Surrey GU21 1GE
■ *Mon-Wed 09:30-18:00, Thu 09:30-20:00, Fri 09:30-18:00, Sat 09:00-18:00, Sun 11:00-17:00*
Separate baby change/feeding room with washbasin.

Big Apple
Crown Square
Woking
Surrey GU21 6HR
01483 727100
■ *Mon-Sun 10:00-23:00, House of Play 10:00-18:00*
Low level children's toilet and baby change area in House of Play.

Boots
1-9 Commercial Way
Woking
Surrey GU21 1YA
■ *Mon-Tue 08:35-17:45, Wed 09:00-17:45, Thu-Sat 08:35-17:45, Sun 11:00-17:00*
Baby change area with washbasin,

feeding section with curtain round and bottle warmer.

Early Learning Centre
19 Commercial Way
Woking
Surrey GU21 1XQ

■ *Mon-Sat 09:00-17:30, Sun 10:00-16:00*

Toilet and separate area with changing mat and chair for feeding.

The Peacocks Centre
Lower Concourse
Woking
Surrey GU21 1GB

■ *Mon-Wed 09:30-18:00, Thu 09:30-20:00, Fri 09:30-18:00, Sat 09:00-18:00, Sun 11:00-17:00*

Separate baby changing room with washbasins and separate feeding room.

Toys'R'Us
Church Street West
Woking
Surrey GU21 1HD
01483 726449

■ *Mon-Fri 09:00-20:00, Sat 09:00-19:00, Sun 11:00-17:00*

Separate baby changing area. Can heat milk at the information desk.

Woking Post Office
Between Commercial Way and Victoria Way
Woking
Surrey GU21 6DG

■ *Open 24 hours*

■ *£0.10*

Automatic public toilet with baby changing facilities.

Wolsey Place Shopping Centre
Middle Walk
Woking
Surrey GU21 1WP
01483 740793

■ *Mon-Sun 09:00-17:30*

Baby change area and toddler strap seat.

Child care & pre-schools

LIVING IN WOKING or the surrounding area means you will have a huge range of childcare providers to choose from, so when it come to making that choice the first thing you need to decide is what type of care will best suit you and your child. Many factors will influence that choice, for example will you be returning to work and so need an all day service, the age of your child will make a difference as not all services are offered for babies, do you prefer your child to be looked after in a group or do you need the flexibilty of a childminder or nanny and so on. We have included a section for each type of care with a brief definition which clarifies the differences between them.

GENERAL INFORMATION

Childcare Link

0800 096 0296 (Helpline)
www.childcarelink.gov.uk

Childcare link provides details of your local information service and fact sheets on your childcare options.

Daycare Trust – The National Childcare Charity

21 St George's Road
London SE1 6ES
020 7840 3350
(Helpline Mon-Fri 10:00-17:00)
www.daycaretrust.org.uk
info@daycaretrust.org.uk

The Daycare Trust works to promote high quality affordable childcare. They offer advice and information on childcare issues.

Surrey Children's Information Service

0845 600 9009
www.surreycc.gov.uk
surrey.cis@surreycc.gov.uk
■ *Mon-Fri 08:00-18:00*

Surrey Children's Information Service can provide information and advice on choosing and paying for early years and childcare, working with children, setting up your own childcare service, training, funding, nursery education grant, special needs, business and other support, childcare for your employees.

CHILDMINDERS

A childminder provides childcare in their own home and is registered and inspected by Ofsted. The child is able to build a warm and trusting relationship with their childminder, which can develop from infancy, through to school age and beyond.

Normally a childminder is registered to care for up to six children under the age of 8, only three of which may be under the age of 5, and usually only one of which may be under the age of 1. These numbers include the childminder's own children. Childminders must be police checked, hold a current first aid certificate and public liability insurance. Some childminders are quality assured, by the Surrey Childminding Network and/or by the NCMA's Quality First Scheme.

It is not possible to list individual childminders, as the list constantly changes, but lists of childminders with vacancies can be obtained from the Children's Information Service (CIS) on 0845 600 9009 or **www.childcarelink.gov.uk**

For more information about Childminders:

National Childminding Association (NCMA)

020 8464 6164
www.ncma.org.uk

Surrey County Childminding Association (SCCMA)

Fiona Howells 01483 772454

Woking Childminding Group

Denise Penhallurick 01483 837005

Chris Ripley (Childminding Project Manager for Surrey)

01932 854656

CRÈCHES

Crèches provide short term childcare and are usually attached to an amenity.

Childcare in the Community

The Maybury Centre
Board School Road
Woking
Surrey GU21 5HD
01483 776877

■ *Mon-Fri 09:30-11:30,*
Mon 13:00-15:00 for Arabic classes,
Wed 12:30-14:30 for friendship group
£2 per session

Multi-cultural crèche available to those receiving training at the Maybury Centre. For children 6mths-5yrs. A large variety of activities provided, small contained outdoor play area. Water and snack provided. Potty training support given. **P**

Camberley Arena Crèche

The Arena Leisure Centre
Grand Avenue
Camberley
Surrey GU15 3QH
01276 65040
www.arenaleisurecentre.co.uk

■ *Mon-Fri 09:00-15:00, Sat 09:15-12:30*

Well equipped crèche available for children aged 0-5yrs for up to 4 hours. Booking advised. **P**

Cannons Health Club Crèche

Cannons Health Club
Pyrford Road
Woking
Surrey GU22 8UQ
01932 351835

■ *Mon 09:15-15:45, Tue 09:15-13:15,*
Wed 09:15-17:00, Thu 09:15-13:15,
Fri 09:15-15:45, Sat 09:15-13:15,
Sun 09:15-12:45

Provides up to 2 hours crèche facilities for Health Club members. The crèche is for up to 19 children aged 12wks-5yrs. Separate baby area. Drinks and snacks provided and will give child lunch if supplied by parent. Potty training support provided.

Guildford Spectrum Leisure Centre Crèche

Parkway
Guildford
Surrey GU1 1UP
01483 443358
www.guildfordspectrum.co.uk
info@guildfordspectrum.co.uk

■ *Mon-Fri 10:00-12:00*

Crèche facilities are available for children aged between 3mths-5yrs. Friendly qualified staff providing a stimulating environment. Booking advised. Crèche hours may be changing in the future – please phone for more details. **P**

River Bourne Health Club Crèche

River Bourne Health Club
Heriot Road
Chertsey
Surrey KT16 9DR
01932 560560

■ *Mon-Fri 09:00-16:00*

Provides up to 2 hours crèche facilities for members and non-members. Crèche is for children aged 3mths-5yrs. Activities include a ball pit and art table. Drinks and snacks provided. Potty training support provided. Access via lift. **P**

Woking Leisure Centre Crèche

Woking Park
Kingfield Road
Woking
Surrey GU22 9BA

01483 771122

■ *Mon-Fri 09:30-11.25*

Children aged 6mths-4yrs11mths are looked after by friendly staff. Crèche is based at the leisure centre but Pool in the Park users are also invited to use this facility. Children under 1yr may not use the crèche if the parent is using the pools. **P**

DAY CARE NURSERIES

Day care nurseries typically offer all day childcare for most of the year for children from 3 months to 5 years.

- All OFSTED inspected
- All provide food/meals
- All have a daily, or part daily fee unless stated otherwise
  Please apply to the nursery for more details
- All have nursery education grant funding available unless otherwise stated
- All cater for Special Educational Needs and English as a Second Language
- All have an indoor play area

Caring Daycare

Blackmore Crescent
Sheerwater
Woking
Surrey GU21 5QJ
01483 729330
www.caringdaycare.co.uk

■ *Mon-Fri 08:00-18:30*

Carer ratio 1:3 0-2yrs, 1:4 2-3yrs, 1:8 3-5yrs

Montessori daycare and education in a safe and stimulating environment to meet the individual needs of the children as they develop. Special community rates available on the fees. **P**

Carol's Montessori Day Nursery

Kitterick
Shaftesbury Road
Woking
Surrey GU22 7DU
01483 740542

■ *Mon-Fri 08:00-18:00*

Carer ratio 1:3

Carol's Montessori Day Nursery is a small, cosy, home-based nursery which is family orientated.

Cherrybrook Nursery

Scotland Bridge Road
New Haw
Surrey KT15 3AQ
01932 336662

■ *Mon-Fri 08:00-18:00*

Carer ratio 1:3 0-2yrs, 1:4 2-3yrs, 1:8 3-5yrs

Cherrybrook Nursery has a wide range of activities including creative, sensory, gross and fine motor skills. There is a large outside play area with a sandpit, climbing frame, bikes and outdoor play equipment.

Cherrylands Nursery

Sopwith Drive
Brooklands Business Park
Weybridge
Surrey KT13 0YU
01932 354175

■ *Mon-Fri 08:00-18:00*

Carer ratio 1:3 0-2yrs, 1:5 2-5yrs

The younger children are involved in plenty of free play including messy play, the older children have a more structured day. There is an outdoor grassed area with a climbing frame and outdoor play equipment.

Christopher Robin Day Nursery

Claremont Avenue
Woking
Surrey GU22 7SF
01483 747131
www.daynurseriessurrey.co.uk

■ *Mon-Fri 08:00-18:00*

Carer ratio 1:3 0-2yrs, 1:4 2-3yrs 1:5/1:6 3-5yrs

Fun, wide range of stimulating activities in a Montessori nursery environment. Fully equipped outdoor play area. Other branches in Burpham, Merrow, Wood Street Village and Cranleigh. **P**

Daydream Nursery

Hillersdon
Horsell Rise
Horsell
Woking
Surrey GU21 4AY
01483 714827

■ *Mon-Fri 08:00-18:00*

Carer ratio 1:3 0-2yrs, 1:4 2-5yrs

Daydream nursery helps children to learn through play in a home from home amosphere. Half acre outside grounds with climbing frame and other equipment. **P**

Doodles II

26 Keston Avenue
New Haw
Surrey KT15 3ES
01932 888342

■ *Mon-Fri 08:00-18:00*

Carer ratio 1:3

Doodles II is a home-from-home environment in which there are a maximum of 6 children. No nursery education grant funding available. Fees are paid by the hour. Outdoor area with sand and water play.
P

First Steps Nursery

St Peters Hospital
Guildford Road
Chertsey
Surrey KT16 0PZ
01932 722192

■ *Mon-Fri 07:00-20:00 for hospital staff, 08:00-18:00 external*

Carer ratio 1:3 0-2yrs, 1:4 2-3yrs, 1:8 3-5yrs

First Steps is a workplace nursery with indoor and outdoor play. Playscheme also runs 13 weeks of year for ages 4yrs-10yrs 11mths. Special rates for nursing staff according to salary band. **P**

Kiddiwinks Day Nursery

Bishop David Brown School
Albert Drive
Sheerwater
Woking
Surrey GU21 5RL

01932 350039
www.kiddiwinkschildcare.co.uk
■ *Mon-Fri 07:30-18:00, part days 08:00-13:00, 13:00-18:00*
Carer ratio 1:3 0-2yrs, 1:4 2-3yrs, 1:7 3-4yrs
Experienced and qualified staff promote play-based learning in a caring, fun and friendly atmosphere. Outdoor play area with wide variety of toys and equipment. No nursery education grant funding. P

Leapfrog Day Nursery

50 Cavell Way
Knaphill
Woking
Surrey GU21 2RQ
01483 797966
www.leapfrogdaynurseries.co.uk
■ *Mon-Fri 07:00-19:00*
Carer ratio 1:3 0-2yrs, 1:4 2-3yrs, 1:8 3-5yrs
Leapfrog provide a number of play areas, with a wide range of activities according to the child's age.
P

Noah's Ark Nursery

Blackhorse Road
Woking
Surrey GU22 0RE
01483 233832
www.noahsark-nursery.co.uk
office@noahsark-nursery .co.uk
■ *Mon-Fri 07:30-18:00*
Carer ratio 1:3 0-2yrs, 1:4 2-3yrs, 1:8 3-5yrs
Noah's Ark nursery has separate areas for different ages. It has an outdoor play area including animals and a nature trail. P

Pennypot Nursery School

Pennypot Lane
Chobham
Surrey GU24 8DH
01276 855886

■ *Mon-Fri 08:00-18:00*

Carer ratio 1:3 0-2yrs,
1:4 2-3yrs, 1:8 3-5yrs

Offers variety of activities to assist ethos of learning through play. Wide range of facilities and three outdoor play areas. ✱ P

Summerfield House Day Nursery

Chertsey Road
Chobham
Surrey GU24 8HF
01276 856556
summerfield100@aol.com

■ *Mon-Fri 08:00-18:00*

Carer ratio 1:3 0-2yrs,
1:4 2-3yrs, 1:8 3-5yrs

Summerfield House Day Nursery has four small groups of children, and a wide range of facilities with dedicated staff. A large garden area with ducks and chickens. ✱ P

Teddies Nursery

15 The Grove
Horsell
Woking
Surrey GU21 4AE
01483 770054
www.teddiesnurseries.co.uk
teddiesnurseries@bupa.com

Mon-Fri 08:00-18:00

Carer ratio 1:3 0-2yrs,
1:4 2-3yrs, 1:6 3-5yrs

Nursery with large purpose built garden. Double buggy and wheelchair access is to the ground floor only. ✱

Toad Hall Nursery

The Old School House
Brox Road
Ottershaw
Surrey KT16 0HH
01932 874286
www.toadhall-nursery.co.uk
ottershaw@toadhall-nursery.co.uk

■ *Mon-Fri 08:00-18:00*
Carer ratio 1:3 0-2yrs, 1:4 2-3yrs, 1:7 3-5yrs
At Toad Hall Nursery children undertake a wide range of activities. There are separate outdoor gardens for the 0-2yrs and 2-5yrs.

NURSE, NANNY, AU PAIR AND BABY SITTING SERVICES

These services provide a range of childcare but are not required to be registered by the Council at present.

Anglo-Czech Au Pair Agency

Bridge Farm Cottage
Knowl Lane
Cranleigh
Surrey GU6 8JW
01483 267091
angloczechaupair@onetel.com

Provide personally interviewed au pairs from the Czech Republic for long and short term placements in Surrey. The agency staff speak both English and Czech to help with long term support.

Au Pair Agency Glogovich
Gransden Cottage
Tydcombe Road
Warlingham
Surrey CR6 9LU
01883 624842
www.au-pair-agency.com
info@au-pair-agency.com

Provides au pairs from a range of European countries. Phone interviews for prospective families can be arranged. Can place au pairs within a few days if required.

Bright Eyes Nanny Agency
11 Gatley Drive
Guildford
Surrey GU4 7JJ
01483 506150
www.brighteyesnannyagency.com
brighteyesnannys@aol.com

Professional agency providing daily and live-in nannies and mothers' helps. Staff available on a full-time and part-time, permanent, temporary or emergency cover basis. All nannies personally interviewed and CRB checked.

Delaney International
Bramble Cottage
Thorncombe Street
Bramley
Surrey GU5 0ND
01483 894300
www.delaney-nannies.com
info@delaney-nannies.com

An employment agency providing daily and live-in nannies, mothers' helps and European au pairs. All nannies are fully qualified.

Family First International
Spiceall
Compton
Guildford
Surrey GU3 1JQ
01483 813323
www.nannyagencyuk.co.uk
info@nannyagencyuk.co.uk

Specialists in the recruitment of qualified nannies and experienced mother's helps mainly from Australia, New Zealand and South Africa.

Fry Staff Consultants
48 Gravel Road
Farnborough
Hampshire GU14 6JJ
01252 540761

Provide professional nannies and other domestic staff. Specialise in matching staff to families. Occasionally able to provide emergency staff.

Home Organisers
Investment House
3/28 Queens Road
Weybridge
Surrey KT13 9UT
01932 844321

Provide nannies, babysitters, mothers' helps, au pairs and cleaners on an emergency or permanent basis.

Hyde Park International Ltd
Belmont House
The Dean
Alresford
Winchester
Hampshire SO24 9BQ
01962 733466
www.hydeparkint.com
info@hyde-park-int.co.uk

Recruitment agency specialising in the provision of nannies, maternity nurses and all other household help.

Jobs in Demand Childcare
www.childcare.org.uk
mail@jobsindemand.com

Based in Knaphill, Woking, local mother, Lynne Ledda has been placing au pairs, nannies and housekeeping staff in the Surrey area for over 4 years, from her home-run business. Offers full-time, part-time and temporary staff and has on-line database search facilities. Candidates are all CRB checked.

Playtime Nanny Agency

55 Queens Road
Knaphill
Woking
Surrey GU21 2ED
01483 488511
www.playtimenannies.co.uk
playtimenannies@btopenworld.com

Provide daily and live-in nannies and mothers' helps. Staff available on a full-time and part-time, permanent, temporary or emergency cover basis. All candidates are personally interviewed, reference checked and have been through the enhanced disclosure procedure.

Safehands Networks Ltd

0870 844 6688
www.safehandsnetwork.com
general@safehandsnetwork.com

Safehands provides a range of services such as babysitting, day care, nanny service, care for children with special needs, mobile crèche facilities (for special events), and also cater for children's birthday parties.

Select Nannies

82 Woodlands Avenue
West Byfleet
Surrey KT14 6AP
01932 402146
www.select-nannies.co.uk
selectnannies@hotmail.com

Provide daily and live-in nannies, on a full-time and part-time, temporary or permanent basis. Also provide maternity nurses and mothers' helps. All nannies personally interviewed and CRB checked.

Sitters

The Call Centre
126 Rickmansworth Road
Watford
Hertfordshire WD18 7WS
0800 389 0038
www.sitters.co.uk
enquiries@sitters.co.uk

Professional babysitting service at set rates depending on your postcode. Booking fee payable each time you use the service.

Surrey Au Pair Agency

Rose Villa
Tuckey Grove
Ripley
Woking
Surrey GU23 6JG

01483 223918
surrey@aupairs-england.com
Provide au pairs from European countries for short and long term placements. All au pairs carefully checked and interviewed.

The Wentworth Nanny Agency
Amboseli
Corrie Gardens
Virginia Water
Surrey GU25 4JH
01344 844597
wentworth.nannies@btopenworld.com
Provide daily and live-in nannies and mothers' helps on a full-time, part-time and temporary basis. Also provide regular babysitters and au pairs. All candidates are interviewed, reference checked and have been through the enhanced disclosure procedure via the CRB.

NURSERY CLASSES ATTACHED TO SCHOOLS

- All OFSTED inspected
- All free unless otherwise stated
- All cater for Special Educational Needs and English as a Second Language
- All classes available to start in term after child's 3rd birthday unless otherwise stated
- All have indoor play area

Chertsey Nursery School
Pyrcroft Road
Chertsey
Surrey KT16 9ER
01932 562225
www.chertsey.surrey.sch.co.uk
head@chertsey.surrey.sch.uk
■ *Mon-Fri 09:00-11:30 or 12:45-15:15, full-time 09:00-14:30*
Carer ratio 3 staff with up to 22 children
Variety of activities to stimulate literacy, numeracy and social skills. Food is provided. Buggies must be left outside, as it is a Grade II listed building. ✱ **P**

Darley Dene Infant School
Garfield Road
Addlestone
Surrey KT15 2NP
01932 847674
www.darley-dene.surrey.sch.uk
■ *Mon-Fri 09:05-11:30 or 12:00-14:55*
40 place nursery which is a part of the school. Well equipped indoor and outdoor areas. Full-time qualified nursery teacher. Children can bring their own fruit, but milk is provided.
✱ **P** ♿

Flexlands School
Station Road
Chobham
Surrey GU24 8AG
01276 857341
www.flexlands.org.uk
■ *Mon-Fri 08:45-11:45 or 12:45-15:15*
■ *£19.80 per session*
Carer ratio 1:8
The nursery class is an integral part of the school. Children are encouraged to work and play co-operatively. Emphasis on positive reinforcement for good behaviour. Large grounds with nature trail and pond. Food is provided. ✱ **P** ♿

Greenfield School
Brooklyn Road
Woking
Surrey GU22 7TP
01483 772525
www.greenfield.surrey.sch.uk

■ *Mon-Fri 08:30-15:15*
■ *5 full days £1,790 per term, 5 mornings £1,065*
Carer ratio 1:5
Nursery class with own outdoor play area with climbing frame and garden equipment. Children start in mornings only, and then gradually increase their time until they are full-time. Nursery grants for 3yr olds available. Bring own packed lunch. P

Halstead Preparatory School for Girls

Woodham Rise
Woking
Surrey GU21 4EE
01483 772682
www.halstead-school.org.uk
registrar@halstead-school.org.uk

■ *Mon-Fri 08:30-15:45*
■ *Cost–apply for details*
Nursery class in which pupils are engaged in purposeful activities in a homely building and grounds. Children start in mornings only and then gradually increase their time until they are attending for full days. Lunch is provided. P

Kingfield School

Kingfield Road
Woking
Surrey GU22 9EQ
01483 761885
admin@kingfield.surrey.sch.uk

■ *Mon-Fri 08:45-11:15 or 12:25-14:50*
■ *Donation requested to cover snacks*
Carer ratio 1:8
Nursery class has two rooms, and an outdoor area. Qualified nursery teacher. Focus for the week is reflected both inside and outside. Snacks are provided. P

Maybury Infant School

Walton Road
Woking
Surrey GU21 5DW
01483 763272
www.maybury.surrey.sch.uk
info@maybury.surrey.sch.uk

■ *Mon-Fri 09:00-11:30 or 12:45-15:15*
Carer ratio 1:10
Nursery curriculum is based on the six areas of learning in the Foundation Stage guidelines. Snacks are provided.

Ripley Court School

Rose Lane
Ripley
Surrey GU23 6NE
01483 225217
www.ripleycourt.surrey.sch.uk
rcshead@btconnect.com

■ *Mon-Fri 08:30-15:25*
■ *£1,830 per term*
Carer ratio 1:8
School and nursery are broadly Christian in philosophy. All children follow the Foundation Stage guidelines. Provides full range of facilities including dancing and swimming. The nursery is for children age $2\frac{1}{2}$ yrs up to school age. Government funding available. P

St Andrew's School

Church Hill House
Horsell
Woking
Surrey GU21 4QW
01483 760943
www.st-andrews.woking.sch.uk

■ *Mon-Fri 08:35-12:30 or 08:45-15:15*
■ *£1,165 per term for 5 part sessions £1,540 per term for 5 full sessions*
Carer ratio 1:8
Nursery has separate playground though pupils have access to larger

grounds under supervision for projects, sports and play opportunities.
P

St Charles Borromeo Catholic School

Portmore Way
Weybridge
Surrey KT13 8JD
01932 842617
head@stcharlesb.surrey.sch.uk

■ *Mon-Fri 09:10-11:40 or 12:40-15:10*
Carer ratio 1:13
School and nursery with Catholic faith. Offers full range of Foundation Stage activities and learning. Has secure outside play area including covered area. **P**

St John's Primary School

Victoria Road
Knaphill
Woking
Surrey GU21 2AS
01483 476450
admin@st-johns-knaphill.surrey.sch.uk

■ *Mon-Fri 09:00-11:30*
Carer ratio 1:13
The nursery class is well planned, and has indoor and outdoor activities. Offers full access to Foundation Stage curriculum. **P**

PRE-SCHOOLS AND PLAYGROUPS

Pre-schools generally offer childcare for less than four hours per day for children from the age of 2 1/2 years to school age.

- All OFSTED inspected
- All cater for children with Special Educational Needs and English as a Second Language
- All have Nursery Education Grant Funding available for 3-4yr olds
- All open term-time only
- All have indoor play area

ABC Pre-School

Westfield Primary School
Bonsey Lane
Westfield
Woking
Surrey GU22 9PR
Mrs Vora 07803 478380

■ *Mon–Fri 09:00-11.30 (3-5yrs), 12:30–15:00 (2 1/2 yrs-3yrs)*
■ *£7.50 per session*
Carer ratio 1:4 2 1/2 yrs, 1:6 3-5yrs
Located in and share good links with primary school. Pushchair/wheelchair access up to door. Outdoor play area with grassed area and outdoor class-room. Drink and snack provided. **P**

The Academy Pre-School

David Lloyd Leisure
Westfield Avenue
Woking
Surrey GU22 9PF
Deborah Dyke 01483 722113

■ *Mon-Fri 09:30-12:00*
■ *£12 member, £14.50 non member per session*
Carer ratio 1:4 under 3yrs, 1:5 3-5yrs
Pre-school with a range of activities, covering all Early Learning Goals. Snacks provided. **P**

Bisley Village Playgroup

Bisley Village Hall
School Close
Bisley
Surrey GU24 9EG
Becky Mills 01483 473947

■ *Mon-Fri 09:15-11:45, 12:15-14:45*
■ *£6 per session*
Carer ratio 1:5
Playgroup with lots of space for indoor play as well as own garden. Milk and biscuits provided. **P**

Blossom Montessori School

St Francis Centre
Pembroke Road
Woking
Surrey GU22 7DY
Pina Consiglio 01483 726040

■ *Mon-Fri 08:45-11:45, 12:30-15:30*
■ *£12 per session*
Carer ratio 1:4 $2\frac{1}{2}$ yrs, 1:8 over 3yrs
One Montessori classroom, one general classroom with mixed activities, one quiet room, and a garden with grass, slide and a sand pit. **P**

Buckles

Holy Family School
Ongar Hill
Addlestone
Surrey KT15 1BP
Mrs Lisa Fuller 01932 827556

■ *Mon-Fri 09:00–11:45, Mon-Thu 12:30–15:00*
■ *£7.50 per session*
Carer ratio 1:5 $2\frac{1}{2}$ yrs, 1:8 over 3yrs
Montessori pre-school with outdoor play area. Different themes explored each term. Drink and snack provided. **P**

Burpham Pre-School

Church of the Holy Spirit
New Inn Lane
Burpham
Surrey GU4 7JH
Jenny Philpot 01483 302635
01483 827413 (home)

■ *Mon-Wed and Fri 09:20–12:00*
■ *Cost per session under review*
Carer ratio 1:6
Large pre-school that follows Stepping Stones curriculum and has use of sports field. Snacks provided. **P**

Busy Beavers Pre-School

Community Centre
Sundridge Road
Old Woking
Surrey GU22 9AT
Karen Smith 01483 763974

■ *Mon–Fri 09:15–12:00*
■ *£5 per session*
Carer ratio 1:8 2yrs, 1:12 3yrs
Pre-school for children aged from 2yrs. Have soft surface outdoor play area. No nursery education grant funding available. Snacks provided. **P**

Crescent Pre-School

Roman Catholic Church
Madeira Road
West Byfleet
Surrey KT13 9DP
Carol Smart 01483 724005

■ *Mon-Fri 09:15–12:45*
■ *£9.50 per session*

Carer ratio 1:8
A large pre-school for children aged from 2yrs. Snack provided.

Discovery Montessori

West Byfleet Infant School
Camphill Road
West Byfleet
Surrey KT14 6EF
Sarah Morton 01932 354284
www.discoverymontessori.co.uk
principal@discoverymontessori.co.uk

■ *Mon-Fri 09:15–12:15, 12:00-15:30 or 13:00-15:30*
■ *Approximately £12 per session*

Carer ratio 1:4 2-3yrs, 1:8 3-4yrs, 1:6/1:8 4-5yrs
A purpose built Montessori nursery school with four classrooms and garden for children aged from 2yrs. Provide range of experiences that will encourage and stimulate child's love of learning. Food is provided.

Downside Nursery

The Old School Room
Downside Road
Downside
Cobham
Surrey KT11 3NA
Chris Griffiths 01932 866556

■ *Mon-Fri 09:00–12:30*
■ *Cost per session varies*

Carer ratio 1:4 2yrs, 1:8 3-5yrs
For children aged from 2yrs. Large outdoor playground.

Humpty Dumpty Pre-School

Holy Trinity Church Hall
Chobham Road
Knaphill
Woking
Surrey GU21 2SX
Mrs Bailey 01483 888465
01483 824006 (Home)

■ *Mon-Fri 09:00-12:00*
■ *£6 per session (due to increase in September 2004)*

Carer ratio 1:6
Pre–school with activities including music and movement, puzzles, painting, craft, playdough, home corner, sand, water play, cooking. Fenced garden for outdoor play. Milk and biscuit provided.

Jack and Jill Pre-School

Sythwood School
Sythwood
Horsell
Woking
Surrey GU21 3AX
Shirley Sparling 01483 767216

■ *Mon-Fri 09:00-11:30, Mon and Wed 12:30-15:00*
■ *£7.50 per session*

Carer ratio – 22 children per session and 4 staff
Aims to provide a safe and secure environment where children learn through play and experience. All children regardless of ability are able to access all areas of curriculum. Outdoor play area with ride on toys, sand, water and climbing frame. The nursery is for children aged from 2yrs.

Jackanory Pre-School

The Youth Centre
Windsor Road
Chobham
Surrey GU24 8NA
Mrs Turner 01276 858634 (Home)
07801 120408 (Mobile)

■ *Tots Room (from 2yrs) Mon-Thu 09:30–12:00, Main Hall (from $2^{1}/_{2}$yrs) Mon-Fri 09:15–12:15*
■ *£8 (tots) £7 (main hall) per session*

Carer ratio 1:4 2yrs, 1:8 $2^{1}/_{2}$yrs
Pre–school for children from 2yrs. Activities include painting, pasting, jigsaws, construction, playdough,

home corner, nature, music, pre-writing and pre-maths. Large outdoor play area. Milk and biscuit provided. Due to move from the Youth Centre to The Community Centre next door. P

Jiminy Cricket Playgroup

Horsell Cricket Pavillion
Brewery Road
Horsell
Woking
Surrey GU21 4QD
Mrs Sheila Rose 01483 768556 (Home)

■ *Mon-Fri 09:15-12:00, Mon-Thu 13:00–15:30*
■ *£7.50 per session*
Carer ratio 1:4 2yrs, 1:8 3-5yrs
Activities include painting, craft sand play, climbing equipment, project work, music and stories. Does not cater for children with English as a second language. Drink and snack provided. P

Linden Nursery School

St Thomas More Church Hall
Binfield Road
Byfleet
Surrey KT14 7PN
Michelle Monan 01932 356361 (Home)
07773 777089 (Mobile)

■ *Mon-Fri 09:15–11:45, Mon-Thu 12:45–14:45*
■ *£8 (mornings), £9 (afternoons)*
Carer ratio 1:4 2½-3yrs, 1:8 3-4yrs
All activities are in line with Early Learning Goals for the Foundation Stage. Large outdoor play area. Drink and snack provided. P

Little Owl Playgroup

Lancaster Hall
28 Send Road
Send
Woking
Surrey GU23 7ET
Catelina Brook 01483 212669 (during playgroup hours)
07729 632552 (Mobile)
www.little-owl-playgroup.co.uk

■ *Mon-Fri 09:15–11.45*
■ *£8 (under 3yrs) £7 (over 3yrs) per session*
Carer ratio 1:4 under 3yrs, 1:6 over 3yrs
For children aged from 2yrs. Children participate in free play, creative and structured activities. Weekly learning topic. Outings for the children and social events for parents and staff are arranged. Snack is provided. No minimum number of sessions. Lunchtime club for the older children. P

Paddington Pre-School

Woking Adult Learning Centre
Highlands
Bonsey Lane
Westfield
Woking
Surrey GU22 9PR
Mrs Sheila Harrison 01483 726480 (Home)
07810 021638 (Mobile)

■ *Mon-Fri 09:00–12:30*
■ *£6 per session*
For children aged from 2yrs. Four fully equipped rooms covering all areas of learning. Fenced outdoor area with climbing frame. Does not cater for children with English as a second language. P

Peter Pan Pre-School Nursery

Tanglewood
Littlewick Road
Lower Knaphill
Woking
Surrey GU21 2JZ
Mrs Sue Lewis 01483 799838 or 488484

lewpy@globalnet.co.uk

■ *Mon-Fri 09:15–12:00, Mon-Tue 12:45–14:45*

■ *£9.50 per session*

Carer ratio 1:5

Pre-school set in woodland. Outdoor play area with covered space. Covers Foundation Stage curriculum. Snack and drink provided.

The Pied Piper Pre-School

The Methodist Church Hall
The Broadway
Knaphill
Woking
Surrey GU21 2DR
Karen Deluce 07946 284636 (Mobile)

■ *Tue, Thu and Fri 09:30-12:00*

■ *£5.50 per session*

Carer ratio 1:6

For children aged from 2yrs. Does not cater for children with special educational needs or with English as a second language. Activities include painting, water, sand, climbing frame, crafts, cooking. Snack provided.
P

Pre-School at St Saviours

St Saviours Church Hall
Connaught Road
Brookwood
Woking
Surrey GU24 0HF
Sally Wells 01483 888531 (09:00–13:00)
01483 834587 (13:00–18:00)

■ *Mon-Fri 09:30–12:00 with additional lunch hour session available*

■ *£8 (2–$2^1/_2$ yrs), £6.50 ($2^1/_2$-4yrs) per session*

Carer ratio 1:4 2yrs, 1:8 3-5yrs plus additional staff

Small room for children up to $2^1/_2$ yrs and a main hall for older children. Activities include creative, IT, role play. Small groups use side room for more structured activities. Drink and snack provided. **P**

Puddle Ducks Tots and Pre-school

St Peters Church Centre
Church Street
Old Woking
Surrey GU22 9JF
Liza Kirby and Carol Hart 01483 874057
07759 127582 (Mobile)
lizakirby@pdpreschool.fsnet.co.uk

■ *Mon-Fri 09:15–12:15 and 12:15–14:45*

■ *£7 (mornings), £6.50 (afternoons) £12 all day*

Carer ratio 1:4

Pre–school following Stepping Stones curriculum. **P**

Red Balloon Pre-School

New Haw Community Centre
Woodham Lane
New Haw
Surrey KT15 3ND
Jackie Hord 07941 392986 (Mobile)
jackiehord@hotmail.com

■ *Mon, Tue and Thu 09:30–12:15*

■ *£8 per session (possible price increase)*

Carer ratio 1:6

Pre-school for children aged from 2yrs. Covers all six learning areas.
P

Spinning Top Pre-School

Sheerwater Youth Centre
Blackmore Crescent
Sheerwater
Woking
Surrey GU21 5NS
Sue Sawyer 07719 753652 (Mobile)

■ *Mon-Fri 08:30–12:30*

■ *£6.50 per $2^1/_2$ hr session*

Carer ratio 1:4 2yrs

For children aged from 2yrs. School drop-off service available. **P** 🚶 🚶 ♿

Sunflower Nursery

Jacobs Well Village Hall
Jacobs Well Road
Guildford
Surrey GU4 7PD
Mrs Balenti 01483 302594 (Home)
01483 560238 (Hall)
07961 100733 (Mobile)

■ *Mon-Thu 09:30–12:15*
■ *£7.70 per session*
Carer ratio 1:4 2yrs, 1:8 3yrs.
For children aged from 2yrs. Activities include stories, singing, group work, counting, drawing, painting, craft. Milk and snack provided. School drop-off service available. ✱ **P** 🚶 🚶 ♿

Tringham Pre-School

Tringham Hall
Benner Lane
West End
Woking
Surrey GU24 9JP
Mrs K J Lewin 01276 856714

■ *Mon-Fri 09:15–11:45*
■ *£6.25 per session*
Carer ratio 1:5
For children aged from 3yrs. Accredited by Pre-school Learning Alliance. Adjacent to playground, village green and pond. Mandarin/ Cantonese speaking teacher on staff. Intakes only from West End, Bisley and Chobham area. ✱ **P** 🚶 🚶 ♿

Wayside Pre-School

Beaufort Primary School
Kirkland Avenue
Goldsworth Park
Woking
Surrey GU21 3RG
Carrie English 07952 401216 (Mobile)
www.wayside-preschool.com

■ *Mon-Fri 09:15–11:30 and 12:45–15:15*
■ *£6.50 per session (discount offered for half-termly payment in advance)*
Carer ratio 1:5 (as a minimum)
Nursery is in grounds of school with own secure playground. All teachers qualified to NVQ level 3. Snack provided. ✱ **P** 🚶 🚶 ♿

Woodlands Pre-School

Barnsbury Infant School
Hawthorn Road
Woking
Surrey GU22 0BA
Michelle Monan 01483 772322
07773 777089 (Mobile)

■ *Mon-Fri 09:00–11:30, Tue and Thu 12:45–14:45*
■ *£7.50 (mornings) £8 (afternoons)*
Carer ratio 1:4 under 3yrs, 1:8 3-4 yrs
Activities are in line with the Early Learning Goals for the Foundation Stage. Small step to access premises. Outdoor playground within school in which pre-school is set. Drink and snack provided. ✱ **P**

Young World Pre-School

Scout HQ
121 High Street
Horsell
Woking
Surrey GU21 4SS
Sue Bullard 01483 770349 (Home)
07774 942627 (Mobile)

■ *Mon-Fri 09:15-12:15*
■ *£7.50 per session*
Carer ratio 1:6
Pre-school with range of activities including structured and free play. No outside area, but second hall for large equipment. Drink and biscuit provided. **P** 🚶 🚶 ♿

Quick Reference Guide to Day Care, Pre-Schools and Nursery Classes

Addlestone, Chertsey, New Haw & Ottershaw
Buckles, Cherrybrook Nursery, Chertsey Nursery School, Darley Dene Infant School, Doodles II, First Steps Nursery, Red Balloon Pre-School, Toad Hall Nursery

Bisley, Brookwood & West End
Bisley Village Playgroup, Pre-School at St Saviour's, Tringham Pre-School.

Brooklands, Cobham & Weybridge
Cherrylands Nursery, Downside Nursery, St Charles Borromeo Catholic School.

Burpham, Jacobs Well, Merrow & Wood Street
Burpham Pre-School, Christopher Robin Day Nursery, Sunflower Nursery.

Byfleet & West Byfleet
Crescent Pre-School, Discovery Montessori School, Linden Nursery School.

Chobham
Flexlands School, Jackanory Pre-School, Pennypot Nursery School, Summerfield House Day Nursery.

Horsell
Day Dream Nursery, Jack and Jill Pre-School, Jiminy Cricket Playgroup, St Andrew's School, Teddies Nurseries, Young World Pre-School.

Kingfield & Westfield
ABC Pre-School, The Academy Pre-School, Kingfield School, Paddington Pre-School.

Quick Reference Guide to Day Care, Pre-Schools and Nursery Classes

Knaphill
Humpty Dumpty Pre-School, Leapfrog Day Nursery, Peter Pan Nursery, The Pied Piper Pre-School.

Old Woking
Busy Beavers Pre-School, Puddle Ducks & Tots Pre-School.

Send & Ripley
Little Owl Playgroup, Ripley Court School.

Sheerwater
Caring Daycare, Kiddiwinks Day Nursery, Spinning Top Pre-School.

Woking, Maybury & St Johns
Blossom Montessori School, Carol s Montessori Day Nursery, Christopher Robin Day Nursery, Greenfield School, Halstead Preparatory School for Girls, Maybury Infant School, St John's Primary School, Wayside Pre-School, Woodlands Pre-School.

Services

THE UNDERLYING theme of this book is to try to make things easier for you as the parent or carer of a young child or baby and this chapter aims to do that by providng information on services where the level of child friendliness really makes a difference when you need to use them. There are two categories of services, those for your child such as hairdressers and party entertainers and community services such as libraries and places of worship.

HAIRDRESSERS

Barbary's
Unit 6
Goldsworth Park Centre
Woking
Surrey GU21 3BA
01483 747420

■ *Mon 09:00-17:30, Tue-Wed 09:00-18:00, Thu-Fri 09:00-19:00, Sat 09:00-17:30, Sun 10:00-16:00*
■ *Cost on a time scale basis*
Child's tractor seat and children's gowns. Toys and books available. Children get a lollipop. P

The Cutting Edge
137 Station Road
Addlestone
Surrey KT15 2AT
01932 828688

■ *Mon-Wed 09:00-18:00, Thu-Fri 09:00-20:00, Sat 09:00-18:00*
■ *£3 for children*
Children's seat and gowns. Some toys available and children get a lollipop.
P

Design Hair
Nina Smithers 07816 986089

■ *From £5 for young child*
Local professional mum who will cut your hair in the comfort of your own home.

J.K.'s Hair Design
43 Dartmouth Avenue
Sheerwater
Woking
Surrey GU21 5PE
01932 342140

■ *Tue-Wed 09:00-17:00, Thu 09:00-18:00, Fri 09:00-19:00, Sat 09:00-17:00*
Selection of toys and books for children. P

Judy - Mobile Stylist
07899 076663

■ *Mon-Tue, Fri*
Provides home haircutting service.

Julia Saunders - Mobile Hairdresser
01932 880883
07904 168002 (Mobile)

■ *Mon-Fri*
Provides home haircutting service.

Macco
4 Old Woking Road
West Byfleet
Surrey KT14 6LW
01932 345541

■ *Tue 09:00-18:00, Wed 09:00-20:00, Thu-Fri 09:00-18:00, Sat 08:00-17:00 £10 for babies and £15 young children*
Children's booster seat and small gowns. Colouring books available.

Supercuts
64 Peacock Centre
Woking
Surrey GU21 6GB
01483 750634

■ *Mon-Fri 09:30-17:00, Sat 09:00-17:00, Sun 11:00-17:00*
■ *£6.95 for child in week, £10.95 for child at weekend*
Booster seats. No need to book, just turn up when child is feeling fairly cooperative.

Tangles Hair Salon
10 Kingfield Road
Woking
Surrey GU22 9EH
01483 761950

■ *Mon-Sat 09:00-17:30*
■ *£5 for young children*
Children's chair and gowns. Some books available. There is a step up into hairdressers. P

LIBRARIES

Libraries are a great way to keep your child supplied with different books, videos or dvds without it costing you a fortune. Anyone who lives, works or studies in Surrey can join the library free of charge. You can join in person at any Surrey library and your library card can be used in any of the 52 libraries in the county. None of the libraries have public toilets but where there is a public toilet nearby we have mentioned it and as food and drink are not allowed there are of course no baby feeding facilities.

Addlestone Library

Church Road
Addlestone
Surrey KT15 1RW
01932 843648
www.surreycc.gov.uk/libraries

■ *Mon 09:30-13:00, 14:00-17:00, Tue-Wed 14:00-17:00, Fri 09:30-13:00, 14:00-17:00, Sat 09:30-13:00, 14:00-16:00*

Talking books, videos, newspapers and magazines available. Internet access and fax services. Hearing loop available. There is a public toilet adjacent to library and free on-road parking in street next to library. **P**

Bagshot Library

63 High Street
Bagshot
Surrey GU19 5AH
01276 473759
www.surreycc.gov.uk/libraries

■ *Tue 14:00-17:00, Thu 10:00-13:00, Fri 12:00-18:00, Sat 09:30-12:30*

Talking books, videos, newspapers and magazines available. Internet access and hearing loop available. Short term parking in road outside library or else free parking in car park next to supermarket a few minutes walk away.

Byfleet Library

High Road
Byfleet
Surrey KT14 7QN
01932 345274
www.surreycc.gov.uk/libraries

■ *Tue 10:00-13:00, 14:00-18:00, Fri 10:00-13:00, 14:00-17:00, Sat 09:30-16:00*

Talking books, videos, newspapers and magazines available. Internet access and fax services. There is also a meeting room for hire. Children's Storytime is every Tue 14:00-14:30. **P**

Chertsey Library

Guildford Street
Chertsey
Surrey KT16 9BE
01932 564101
www.surreycc.gov.uk/libraries

■ *Mon 10:00-13:00, 14:00-17:00, Tue 14:00-20:00, Thu 14:00-17:00, Fri 10:00-13:00, 14:00-17:00, Sat 09:30-13:00, 14:00-16:00*
Talking books and videos. Internet access and fax services available. Has a few free parking spaces at the rear plus adjacent Borough Council car park in which charges apply.
P

Guildford Library

77 North Street
Guildford
Surrey GU1 4AL
01483 568496
www.surreycc.gov.uk/libraries

■ *Mon 09:30-20:00, Tue 09:30-17:00, Wed 09:30-13:00, Thu 09:30-17:00, Fri 09:30-20:00, Sat 09:30-16:00*
Books, talking books, videos, DVDs, music CDs, Playstation games, newspapers and magazines. Internet access and fax services. Has a Learning Centre and an European Information Centre. Children's Storytime is on Fridays 14:15-14:45 in the Children's Space. There is wheelchair and double buggy access to ground floor and children's area. Council toilet facilities across road from library. No on-site parking but public car parks close by.

Horsley Library

Station Parade
Ockham Road South
East Horsley
Surrey KT24 6QR
01483 283870
www.surreycc.gov.uk/libraries

■ *Tue-Wed 10:00-13:00, 14:00-17:00, Fri 10:00-13:00, 14:00-19:00, Sat 09:30-13:00, 14:00-16:00*
Books, videos, music CDs, talking books, newspapers and magazines. Internet access and fax services. Children's Storytime is every Wed 14:15-14:45. Parking is available in the parade of shops or in parking spaces behind the shops across from the library. **P**

Knaphill Library

High Street
Knaphill
Woking
Surrey GU21 2PE
01483 473394
www.surreycc.gov.uk/libraries

■ *Tue 10:00-13:00, 14:00-19:00, Fri 10:00-13:00, 14:00-17:00, Sat 09:30-13:00, 14:00-16:00*
Books, videos, talking books, newspapers and magazines is available. Internet access and fax services. Council toilet facilities are available across the road and there is free parking a few minutes walk from the library in Queen's Road Car Park.
P

Lightwater Library

83a Guildford Road
Lightwater
Surrey GU18 5SB
01276 452587
www.surreycc.gov.uk/libraries

■ *Tue 14:00-17:00, Fri 10:00-13:00 and 14:00-17:30, Sat 09:30-12:30*
Books, videos, talking books, magazines and newspapers available. Internet access. The library is approached by footpath from High Street with some free parking at the nearby shops.**P**

New Haw Library

The Broadway
New Haw
Surrey KT15 3HA
01932 343091
www.surreycc.gov.uk/libraries

■ *Mon-Tue 10:00-12:30, 14:00-17:00, Thu 14:00-17:00, Fri 10:00-12:30, 14:00-17:00, Sat 09:30-13:00, 14:00-16:00*

Books, videos, talking books, jigsaws, newspapers and magazines available, as well as internet and fax services. Also has a Learning Centre. Free parking available at the nearby shopping parade. **P**

West Byfleet Library

The Corner
West Byfleet
Surrey KT14 6NY
01932 343955
www.surreycc.gov.uk/libraries

■ *Tue 10:00-17:00, Thu 10:00-18:00, Fri 10:00-17:00, Sat 09:30-16:00*

Books, videos, DVDs, talking books, newspapers and magazines. Internet access and fax services available. Children's Storytime is every Tuesday during term time 14:15-14:45. The library is sited within a Borough Council car park in which charges apply.

Weybridge Library

Church Street
Weybridge
Surrey KT13 8DE
01932 843812
www.surreycc.gov.uk/libraries

■ *Mon 10:00-17:00, Tue 10:00-20:00, Wed 10:00-13:00, Fri 10:00-20:00, Sat 09:30-16:00*

Books, videos, DVDs, music CDs, talking books, CD Roms, newspapers and magazines. Internet access and fax services available. Also has a Learning Access Point and European Information Centre. Children's Storytime is on the first and third Tuesday of the month 14:15-14:45. Toilets are available upstairs when the museum is open via a lift. There is a Borough Council car park in which charges apply behind the library.

Woking Library

Gloucester Walk
Woking
Surrey GU21 1HL
01483 770591 (Library)
01483 771011 (Information Centre)
www.surreycc.gov.uk/libraries

■ *Mon 09:30-20:00, Tue-Wed 09:30-17;00, Thu-Fri 09:30-20:00 and Sat 09:30-17:00*

Talking books, videos, DVDs, music CDs, newspapers and magazines available. Internet access and fax services. Also has a Learning Centre and European Information Centre. Children's Storytime is every Wednesday at 11:00. There are toilet and baby changing facilities in the nearby Peacock shopping centre and parking is available in town centre car parks in which charges apply.

TOY LIBRARIES

National Association of Toy and Leisure Libraries

020 7255 4600
www.natll.org.uk

Toy libraries offer services to local families based on regular toy loans for a nominal fee or sometimes for free. They provide carefully selected toys to borrow, play sessions and a friendly, informative meeting place for parents and carers. For information about your local toy library telephone the number above.

Addlestone Toy Library

www.toylib.net

This facility is used by those who live in the borough of Runnymede and those who have children with Special Needs, wherever they live. For further details see the Special Needs section of this book.

NAPPY SERVICES

There is a wide selection of nappy services available today offering both convenience and the ability to help the environment.

Boots

Local branches in Woking, West Byfleet, Weybridge & Guildford

www.boots.co.uk

Website is a source of information on real nappies. Suppliers of nappies and accessories on line and some lines available in store locally.

Cotton Bottoms

7-9 Water Lane Industrial Estate
Water Lane
Stoughton
West Sussex RN20 3XX
0870 777 8899

www.cottonbottoms.co.uk

Offers advice, information or details of local stockists. Sells own products and accessories on-line. Nappy laundering service in GU & KT postcode areas.

Little Naturals

Jessamine Cottage
12 George Road
Milford
Surrey GU8 5HA
01483 427344

www.littlenaturals.co.uk

Offers advice and information. Sells a wide range of nappies and accessories.

Mothercare World

The Paddock Retail Park
Sopwith Way
Brooklands
Weybridge
Surrey KT13 0XF
01932 355069

www.mothercare.com

Stockists of Kooshies range and traditional terries nappies and accessories in store or on-line.

National Association of Nappy Services

0121 693 4949
www.changeanappy.co.uk
A source of information on real nappies and laundering.

Nifty Nappies

Margaret Bell
62 Anstey Road
Alton
Hampshire GU34 2RF
01420 549659
www.niftynappies.co.uk
Nappy supply and laundering service.

The Real Nappy Association

PO Box 3704
London SE26 4RX
01342 843535
www.realnappy.com
A source of information and advice on real nappies, including home washing or laundry services.

Real Nappy Exchange

c/o WEN PO Box 30626
London E1 1TZ
020 7481 9004
www.wen.org.uk/nappies/
nappies@wen.org.uk
To buy nappies, Orla can be contacted on Thursday or Friday only. She will tell you what is currently available. Emailed details will be passed on to buyers. There is no charge for this service, though donations are always welcome. Buyers and sellers negotiate terms and conditions between themselves.

Toys'R'Us

Church Street West
Woking
Surrey GU21 1HD
01483 726449
www.toysrus.co.uk
■ *Mon-Fri 09:00-20:00, Sat 09:00-19:00, Sun 11:00-19:00*
Stockists of Bambino Mio range of nappies in store or on-line.

Woking Borough Council

Civic Offices
Gloucester Square
Woking
Surrey GU21 6YL
01483 755855
www.woking.gov.uk/environment/greenpages/children/parents
■ *Mon-Fri 09:00-16:45*
Provides some information on nappy services.

PARTY ENTERTAINMENT

Angel Event Management

9 Abbey Road
Virginia Water
Surrey GU25 4RS
01344 845966
info@angelevents.co.uk
■ *Mon-Fri*
Offers party planning and agency service for providing entertainers, catering for children of all ages. Typical cost is £250 for event management. Contact Rayna Angel.

Ballooning Mad

1 Cresswell Corner
Anchor Hill
Knaphill
Woking
Surrey GU21 2JD
01483 486100
07957 464013 mobile
www.ballooningmad.com

■ *Mon-Fri 09:30-17:30, Sat 09:00-17:30*
Professional balloon decorators and party shop. Stocks partyware for all occasions including children's themes. All ages catered for - no minimum order - items from 20p. Visit the website to view portfolio of ideas.

Balloons and Costumes

21 High Road
Byfleet
Surrey KT14 7QH
01932 345003

■ *Mon-Fri 08:30-17:30, Sat 08:30-16:30, Sun 08:00-23:00*
Offer balloons for parties, weddings and corporate events. Also has banners and tableware for parties. Sells children's fancy dress and has fancy dress hire for adults. Sells wigs, hats and other accessories. All ages catered for. Typical cost of a child's outfit is £10-£20.

Best of Magic

30 Falkner Court
South Street
Farnham
Surrey GU9 7RF
01252 713183

■ *Available to contact any time.*
'Naughty Nicky' Ward is a children's comedy entertainer. His show features magic, balloon modelling and his puppet 'Charley Crow'. Party programmes can include close-up magic, mini disco, games and competitions. Caters for children age 3yrs upwards. He is a member of the Magic Circle and Silver Star. Typical cost of a full party is £150.

Boing Bouncy Castles

16 Grange Road
Guildford
Surrey GU2 9PY
0845 644 5569
07721 992078 mobile
www.boingcastles.com
julie@boingcastles.com

For children up to 14yrs. Hire of bouncy castles, slides, fun-runs, soft play and mini marquees. Cost from £50.

Catherine's Magic Entertainment

102 Sheep Walk
Shepperton
Middlesex TW17 0AN
01252 837885
07005 394122 mobile
www.magicentertainment.co.uk
catherine@magicentertainment.co.uk

Magic and entertainment suitable for all ages, with shows tailored to suit the requirements of the clients. Also offers 'K T Klown', mini disco, face painting, pass the parcel and other games. Catherine is a member of the Magic Circle. Shows vary in cost but are ideal for parties, fetes or corporate events.

Face the Paint

Grove Barrs
South Road
Horsell
Woking
Surrey GU21 4JN
01483 766244
07860 841494 mobile

For children age 3yrs upwards. Mary Tibbotts is available on Fridays, Saturdays and Sundays for bookings. A professional TV make up artist who provides facepainting for children's parties, school fetes, carnivals, corporate events and promotions. Also offers make up and special effects parties.

GoodTimes

4 Ockenden Gardens
Woking
Surrey GU22 7LY
01483 762501
goodtimespartyplanning@fsmail.net

A service that can design, plan and host a party at home or alternative venues. Offer a formulated party service for nursery age children at some local fitness centres and specialise in themed parties, including entertainers and food, for every age. Can also arrange for face painters, craft parties and bouncy castles. Cost of parties depends on features required.

Hullaballoon

The Studio
Woodham Park Road
Woodham
Surrey KT15 3TG
07977 707857 mobile
www.hullaballoon.co.uk

■ *Wed-Sat 10:00-16:30*

Provide everything you need for a party such as balloons, bouncy castles, pinatas, tableware and a full range of party goods and gifts.

Jayengee Enterprises

21 Ivydene
Knaphill
Woking

Surrey GU21 2TA
01483 836124
07736 101889 mobile
www.jayengee.co.uk

Available for bookings at any time. For children age 2-12 yrs. Bouncy castles and Giant Games for indoor and outdoor use available for hire. Also offers balloons, greeting cards and cake decorations for sale. The typical cost of the bouncy castle is £55 and the Giant Games are around £20 each per day. Free delivery to addresses in the Woking area.

Jelly Kelly

28 Highfield Road
Chertsey
Surrey KT16 8BU
01932 706273
07929 361597 mobile
www.jellykelly.co.uk
jellykelly@wantthebest.fsnet.co.uk

For children 3-8yrs. They provide young, fun and interactive magic shows. Balloon modelling provided. Also offer party games such as musical bumps, musical statues and dressing up race.

Karting Kapers

12 Farnham Park Drive
Hale
Farnham
Surrey GU9 0HS
01252 722358
01252 722358 fax
07799 433830 mobile
mandegoulding@lineone.net

■ *Always open for bookings*

Go-karting parties for children age 4-9yrs cost from £140 and include a medal and photograph for the winner and certificates for all participants. Will also cater for other events such as fetes, shows, family gatherings, fun days and corporate events where the cost is £100 for the first hour and £60 for each extra hour. Bouncy castle hire also available.

Little Blisters

2 South Lodge
59 Ham Common
Richmond
Surrey TW10 7JL
020 8948 3874
07885 663885 mobile
www.childrensentertainment-surrey.co.uk

For children age 3-7yrs. Available anytime. Little Blisters has three popular entertainers: Flossie-Bella the Fairy, Sea Lily the Mermaid and Kitty Willow the Magical Cat. Each of these characters present an interactive show including conjuring tricks, songs, dances, balloon modelling, games and face-painting.

Magic With A Twist

19 Charlock Way
Burpham
Guildford
Surrey GU1 1YB
01483 455997
07714 236082 mobile

For children 3 yrs and upwards. Available anytime and anywhere, providing special magical entertainment for special people. The show features Scruff the Magic Dog, the children's favourite, lots of fun and balloon modelling.

Minnie's Bounce About

21 Oakwood Road
St John's
Woking
Surrey GU21 8UU
01483 487994
www.minnies.net

■ *Mon-Sun 09:00-18:00*
For children up to 14yrs. Hires out ball ponds, soft play and ball pits. Also bouncy castles and slides of various sizes with shower covers. Free local delivery provided plus special rates during Oct-Mar when in a hall. Prices start from £30.

Non Stop Party Shop Ltd

Unit 1 Glenville Mews
Kimber Road
London SW18 4NT
020 8875 1626
www.nonstopparty.co.uk
■ *Mon-Sat 09:00-17:30*
For children up to 10yrs.
Offers comprehensive range of party products under one roof. Can also deliver tables and chairs, bouncy castles and balloons. They have branches in Cobham, Weybridge and Guildford.

Paintbox Faces for Fun

11 Robin Hood Crescent
Knaphill
Woking
Surrey GU21 2NB
01483 487402
For children age 4-9yrs. Provide children's entertainment, professional face-painting, balloon modelling, fancy dress parties and party bags. Typical cost is £50 for painting the faces of 15 children.

The Party Company

142 High Street
Godalming
Surrey GU7 1AB
01483 424542
www.thepartycompany.co.uk
info@thepartycompany.co.uk
■ *Tue-Sat 09:30-17:00*
For children of all ages. A retail shop and mail order company offering a complete range of themed tableware, party boxes, pinatas, party bag toys, helium balloons, decorations and children's fancy dress. Free catalogue available.

Party in a Box Direct

7 Falconwood
East Horsley
Surrey KT24 5EG
01483 286859
www.partyinaboxdirect.co.uk
info@partyinaboxdirect.com
For children age 3-8yrs. Everything you need for the perfect themed party, boxed and delivered to your door. Pirates, princesses, fairies, mermaids and knights as well as mixed themed parties.

Punch and Judy Shows

Flat 7 Woodview Court
8 Queens Road

Weybridge
Surrey KT13 9XF
01932 845589

For children 3-7 years. Traditional Punch and Judy shows, magic and games. Typical cost is £55-75.

Tuneful Tots Magic and Music Parties

01932 224573

Available 7 days a week for magic and music parties. Party entertainment includes a box of magic tricks, musical and percussion instruments, popular songs and a puppet called 'Rocky the Dog'. Children are encouraged to participate. The birthday child receives a cassette as a present. Typical cost for a 1hr booking is £80-£100.

PLACES OF WORSHIP

Woking is is a very diverse community and its places of worship reflect that, there really is something for everyone. However we have not attempted to list something for everyone but have restricted the entries in this section to those places of worship who really welcome children and offer specific services aimed at children and/or Sunday schools or creche's as always the time of services can change so its always a good idea to check before you attend for the first time.

All Saints Church, Woodham

564 Woodham Lane
Woking
Surrey GU21 5SU
01483 727835
woodham@fish.co.uk

■ *Sun 09:45 Parish Eucharist*
Church of England

During the Sunday Parish Eucharist there is a Sunday school and a Play corner is available at the rear of the church. **P**

All Souls Church, Sutton Green

New Lane
Sutton Green
Woking
Surrey GU4 7QF
01483 762707

■ *Sun 09:30 Service*
Church of England
The first Sunday in the month is a Family Service and a Sunday club is held for school age children on the last Sunday of the month. **P**

Church of the Good Shepherd

Coldharbour Road
Pyrford
Woking
Surrey GU22 8SP
01932 349558
01932 356166 (Children Services and Youth Worker)

■ *Sun 10:00 service*
Church of England
The Sunday morning service offers a crèche facility and a Sunday school. There is also a regular Family Service but for more details check the monthly church magazine. Children always welcome. Rooms are available for hire forchildren's birthday and baptism parties. **P**

The Coign Church

Church Street West
Woking
Surrey GU21 6DJ
01483 714150
www.coign.org
welcome@coign.org

■ *Sun 09:00 and 10:45 services with Sunday school*
This is a Christian church which has a crèche and Sunday school at both the Sunday morning services. Also has the Genesis group for families with children with special needs.

Emmanuel Chapel

18 Portugal Road
Woking
Surrey GU21 5JE
01483 835240 (Mr. David Fowler)
familiesarewelcome@emmanuelchapel.co.uk

■ *Wed 17:45-19:00 Junior club (7-11 yrs), Sun 10:00-11:30 Family Worship with Sunday Club*
This is a Christian non-denominational church with a friendly group for all ages on Sundays at 10:00. Small car park on site and plenty of street parking near by. **P**

The Guildford and District Jewish Community Synagogue

York Road
Guildford
Surrey
07939 594212
guildfordjewishcommunity@yahoo.co.uk
www.geocities.com/guildfordjewishcommunity

■ *09:30 Last Saturday in the month religious service*
They have weekly children's cheder classes and children are welcome in the synagogue. Off-road parking available but further parking possible in the car park opposite.
P

Holy Trinity Church

Chobham Road
Knaphill
Woking
Surrey GU21 2SY
01483 473489

■ *Sun 10:30 service with creche and Sunday school, Family service on the first Sunday in the month*
Church of England
Toddler's Praise in the adjoining church once a term lasting about 10 minutes. On street parking also available when car park is full.
P

Horsell Evangelical Church

High Street
Horsell
Woking
Surrey GU21 4SZ
01483 767531

■ *Sun 11:00-12:00 morning worship with creche and Sunday school and 18:30 Sunday evening worship*
Affiliation and fellowship of independent evangelical churches. Children always welcome. **P**

Knaphill Methodist Church

Broadway
Knaphill
Woking
Surrey GU21 2DR
01483 472524

■ *Sun 10:30 Family Service*
Regular Family Church Services are held on a Sunday morning and offer a crèche facility and Junior Church Sunday school. There are all age services once a month and Sunday evening services too. Check the Service details on the notice board outside the church. There is a large car park behind the church with vehicle access at the side of the Co-op. The

Church and all its premises will be closed for approximately 6 months for a redevelopment project from May 2004 onwards. For further information and alternative venues see details outside the church premises.

Meadrow Unitarian Chapel

Meadrow
Godalming
Surrey GU7 3JB
01483 414878
01483 414878 fax
www.unitariangodalming.org.uk
margaret@owen-home.freeserve.co.uk to request the Monthly Newsletter

■ *Family services are Sun 11:00 every second and fourth Sunday in the month*
Every other month one of these services is entirely child-centred. Regular church services and activities for children. The bi-monthly Family Service is followed by a lunch. The Hall and activities are always available for children during services. Naming and blessing services are held for children. Further car parking spaces available opposite premises if car park is full.

Send Evangelical Church

Broadmead Road
Send
Woking
Surrey GU23 7AD
01483 473396
www.sendec.org

■ *Sun 11:00 and 18:30 Sunday services*
Non–denominational Christian church
Crèche available at morning service and children always welcome at either service. The Sunday school is held term-time from 09:40 to 10:40 for children aged 5-10 years, and follows a structured teaching programme.

St. Andrew's Church

Denton Way
Goldsworth Park
Woking
Surrey GU21 3LG
01483 723879

■ *Family Service Sun 10:00, Toddler Service second Wednesday in the month at 10:30*
Ecumenical church
During the Toddler Service there is 20 minutes of music, craft and fun. The Family Service also has a crèche facility and a Sunday school. There is also a popular coffee shop attached which is open Tue-Fri from 10:00-14:00. There is a lift to the worship area and parking available in Waitrose car park.

St. Andrew's United Reformed Church

White Rose Lane
Woking
Surrey GU22 7HA
01483 765568

■ *Sun 10:30 creche and Junior Church during Morning Worship Service*
All children are welcome at the Sunday morning service and there is a crèche facility and Junior Church at the same time. Further parking also available in public car park behind the church.

St. Hugh of Lincoln Catholic Church

95 Victoria Road
Knaphill
Woking
Surrey GU21 2AA
01483 472404

■ *Sat 18:15, Sun 09:30 and weekly Mass at 11:30*
At the 09:30 and 11:30 Mass there is a Children's Liturgy. P

St. Lawrence Chobham

High Street
Chobham
Surrey
01276 858197
www.chobhamchurch.co.uk
andrew@abody.freeserve.co.uk

■ *Sun 08:00 and 10:00 services, Thu 10.45 Parent and toddler service usually on third Thu of month (check Church Notice Board)*
Church of England
Children always welcome and at the 10:00 Sunday service there is a Young Pilgrims group for children age 3yrs and over and also a crèche facility. Regular Parenting group for parents with children under 5yrs. The church has a library of children's books. Special services for children under 5yrs are held on Easter Eve and on Christmas Eve. Parking is available in public car park 200 yards from the church. P

St. Mark's Church of England Church

66 Westfield Road
Woking
Surrey GU22 9NG
01483 770779
iantweediesmith@waitrose.com

■ *Sun 11:00 Sunday service with a Sunday school*
The first Sunday in the month is a Family Service. The other Sunday services have a Sunday school for children age 2-5yrs and a crèche facility is available for babies.
P

St. Mary's Church, Horsell

Church Hill
Horsell
Woking
Surrey GU21 4QQ
01483 772134
www.stmarys-horsell.org.uk
rjones2558@aol.com

■ *Sun 10:00 Communion Service*
There is a crèche facility available at this service and for children age 3-9yrs there is a Sunday school called JAM (Jesus And Me). Parking is available in Horsell Village School car park on Sundays. Pushchair and wheelchair access coming from the back of the Church to the front as at the front there are steep steps up from the road.

St. Mary of Bethany Church

Mount Hermon Road
Woking
Surrey GU22 7UH
01483 723424
www.stmaryofbethany.org.uk

■ *Sun 09:30 and 11:00 services*
Both these Sunday services offer a crèche facility and also have a Sunday school. P

St. Michael's Church

Dartmouth Avenue
Sheerwater
Woking
Surrey GU21 5PJ
01932 341694
stmike@fish.co.uk

■ *Sun 10:30 service*
Anglican/Methodist church
There is a Sunday school held during the Sunday service except on the first Sunday of the month which is a Family Service. P

St. Nicholas' Church

Church Hill
Pyrford
Woking
Surrey GU22 8XH
01932 349558

Church of England
Small and old church (capacity 90). For times of Sunday services check details in monthly church magazine. The Old School Room next to church is also for hire. Toilets are in Old School Room.

St. Paul's Church

Oriental Road
Maybury
Woking
Surrey GU22 7BD
01483 772081
www.stpaulschurch_woking.tripod.com
stpauls.church@btopenworld.com

■ *Sun 08:00 Holy Communion (first and fifth Sundays of the month), 10:30 Family service, Holy Communion or Morning Prayer depending on which Sunday in the month, 18:30 Evening Worship (every Sunday except third when there is Holy Communion)*
Church of England
A Sunday school is available during 10:30 service except during Family Service and there is also a crèche facility. Some parking on site but ample available in the Lion Retail Park opposite.

Wisley Church

Wisley
Surrey
01932 349558

Church of England
Wisley Friends' Room for hire. For details of the services please check the monthly church magazine. Toilet facilities available in Friends' Room.

York Road United Reformed Church

York Road
Woking
Surrey GU22 7XH
01483 727167
www.wokingurc.org.uk

■ *Sun 10:45 service, evening services as announced*
During morning service there is a crèche facility for under 3's and Junior Church for over 3's after first 20 minutes of service. Children very welcome.

Health & Welfare

THIS CHAPTER is intended to be a mini directory of contact points for a wide range of child and family related support groups, medical services including mainstream NHS facilities and complementary or alternative therapies, local support for children with special needs and quite a bit more. So if you are new to the area and need a pharmacy in a hurry or perhaps need someone to talk to about coping with a new baby, its in here.

HEALTH

CHILD HEALTH CLINICS

These clinics are run by Health Visitors. You may attend at any time during the clinic open hours without an appointment. You can have the baby or child up to age 5 weighed and discuss progress or problems with the Health Visitor.

Chobham Surgery

Windsor Road
Chobham
Surrey GU24 8NA
01276 857117

■ *Mon 13:30-15:00*

Goldsworth Park Health Centre

Denton Way
Goldsworth Park
Woking
Surrey GU21 3LQ
01483 728201

■ *Mon 14:00-16:00, Thu 10:00-12:00*

The Maybury Centre

Board School Road
Maybury
Woking
Surrey GU21 5HD

■ *Thu 13:30-15:30*

Parking is limited.

St Johns Health Centre

Hermitage Road
St Johns
Woking
Surrey GU21 1TD
01483 723451

■ *Wed 14:00-16:00, Thu 14:00-16:00*

Parking is limited.

St Michael's Church Hall

Dartmouth Avenue
Sheerwater
Woking
Surrey GU21 5PJ

■ *Tue 11:00-12:30*

The Vyne Community Centre

45 Broadway
Knaphill
Woking
Surrey GU21 2SP

■ *Tue 14:00-16:00*

West Byfleet Health Centre

Madeira Road
West Byfleet
Surrey KT14 6DH
01932 340411

■ *Thu 09:30-11:30*

West End Surgery

Lucas Green Road
West End
Woking
Surrey GU24 9LU
01483 481323

■ *Wed 13:30-15:00*

Woking Community Hospital

Children's Unit
Heathside Road
Woking
Surrey GU22 7HS
01483 715911

■ *Wed 14:00-16:00*

First Mon in month 17:00-19:00 (Second if a Bank Holiday)

QUICK REFERENCE GUIDE TO CHILD HEALTH CLINICS		
	mornings	**afternoons**
Mon		Chobham 13:30–15:00 Goldsworth Park 14:00-16:00 Woking Community Hospital (first Mon in mth) 17:00-19:00
Tue	St Michael's Sheerwater 11:00-12:30	The Vyne Centre Knaphill 14:00-16:00
Wed	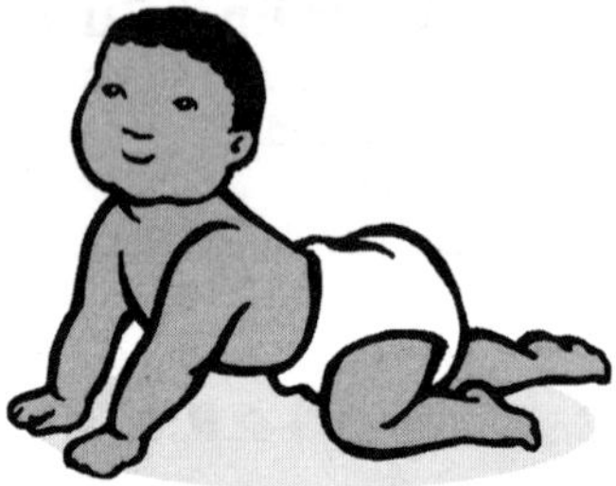	St John's 14:00-16:00 West End 13:30-15:00 Woking Community Hospital 14:00-16:00
Thu	Goldsworth Park 10:00-12:00 West Byfleet 09:30-11:30	The Maybury Centre 13:30-15:30 St John's 14:00-16:00

Please contact your Health Visitor or GP surgery for more information about these clinics.

CHILD WELFARE

Baby Check Ltd

PO Box 324
Worxham
Norwich NR12 8EQ
01603 784400

A booklet developed with funding from the Foundation for the Study in Infant Death with 19 simple checks to help carers interpret how ill a baby under six months actually is and whether you should be consulting a doctor.

National Society for the Prevention of Cruelty to Children (NSPCC)

Weston House
42 Curtain Road
London EC2A 3NH
0808 800 5000 (24hr Helpline)
www.nspcc.org.uk
help@nspcc.org.uk

The NSPCC works to prevent cruelty to children. Their 24hr child protection helpline provides information, advice and counselling to anyone concerned about a child's safety.

COMPLEMENTARY AND ALTERNATIVE THERAPIES

Professional Associations

The Royal Society for the Promotion of Health (RSPH)

38a St George's Drive
London SW1V 4BH
020 7630 0121
www.rsph.org
rshealth@rshealth.org.uk

RSPH is the UK's largest and longest established public health organisation, promoting continuous improvements in human health through education, communication and the encouragement of scientific research. Bookshop available on-line.

Institute for Complementary Medicine (ICM)

PO Box 194
London SE16 1QZ
020 7237 5165
www.icmedicine.co.uk
info@icmedicine.co.uk

ICM provides information on complementary medicine, healing and courses. You can find local practitioners on the website. (See below for more information on specific disciplines)

The Guild of Complementary Practitioners (GCP)

Liddell House
Liddell Close
Finchampstead
Berkshire RG40 4NS
0118 973 5757
www.gcpnet.com
info@gcpnet.com

The Guild is the UK's largest multidisciplinary Association for Professional Therapists. You can find local practitioners on the website. (See below for more information on specific disciplines)

Acupuncture

Acupuncture is a system of healing which has been practised in China and other Eastern countries for centuries. Used to treat people with a wide range of illnesses. Its focus is on improving the overall well being of the patient, rather than the isolated treatment of specific symptoms. Massage or tapping with a rounded probe are techniques particularly suitable for small children or for people with a fear of needles.

British Acupuncture Council
63 Jeddo Road
London W12 9HQ
020 8735 0400
www.acupuncture.org.uk
info@acupuncture.org.uk

The British Acupuncture Council is the UK's main regulatory body for the practice of acupuncture. It maintains standards of education, ethics, practice and discipline, promoting research and enhancing the role that acupuncture can play. You can find local practitioners on the website.

British Medical Acupuncture Society
BMAS House
3 Winnington Court
Winnington Street
Northwich
Cheshire CW8 1AQ
01606 786782
01925 730727
www.medical-acupuncture.co.uk
admin@medical-acupuncture.co.uk

BMAS is an association of medical practitioners who use acupuncture in hospital or general practice. BMAS promotes use of acupuncture as a therapy following orthodox diagnosis. You can find local practitioners on the website.

Aromatherapy

Aromatherapy is the use of essential oils in holistic treatments to improve physical and emotional well-being. Essential oils, extracted from plants, are utilised to improve health and prevent disease. These natural plant oils are applied in a variety of ways, massage (most used method), baths and inhalations (not for asthmatics). Aromatherapy can be especially helpful for stress related conditions.

Aromatherapy Consortium
PO Box 6522
Desborough
Kettering
Northants NN14 2YX
0870 774 3477
www.aromatherapy-regulation.org.uk
info@aromatherapy-regulation.org.uk

The Aromatherapy Consortium acts as a governing body for associations connected to aromatherapy. You can find local therapists on the website.

Chiropractic

Chiropractors treat problems with your joints, bones and muscles, and the effects they have on your nervous system. Working on all the joints of your body, concentrating particularly on the spine, they use their hands to make often gentle, specific adjustments (the chiropractic word for manipulation) to improve the efficiency of your nervous system and release your body's natural healing ability. Chiropractic does not involve the use of any drugs or surgery and can help children with conditions such as asthma, colic, sleep and feeding problems, breathing difficulties, hyperactivity and frequent infections.

The British Chiropractic Association
Blagrave House
17 Blagrave Street
Reading
Berkshire RG1 1QB
0118 950 5950
www.chiropractic-uk.co.uk

enquiries@chiropractic-uk.co.uk
The BCA promotes chiropractic education, patient care, standards of practice and continuous professional development. You can find local practitioners on the website.

Herbal Medicine

Medical Herbalists are trained in the same diagnostic skills as orthodox doctors but take a more holistic approach to illness. The underlying cause of the problem is sought and, once identified, it is this which is treated, rather than the symptoms alone. Herbalists are able to treat a wide range of conditions both acute and chronic in nature and treatment may include advice about diet and lifestyle as well as herbal medicine.

National Institute of Medical Herbalists

56 Longbrook Street
Exeter
Devon EX4 6AH
01392 426022
www.nimh.org.uk
nimh@ukexeter.freeserve.co.uk
The NIMH studies and researches the practice of herbal medicine. You can find local practitioners on the website.

Homeopathy

Homeopathy is a system of healing which assists the natural tendency of the body to heal itself. It recognises that all symptoms of ill health are expressions of disharmony within the whole person and that it is the patient who needs treatment not the disease. Homeopathic medicine is safe for mothers to be and children as it cannot cause side effects and you cannot become addicted to them. This is because only a very minute amount of the active ingredient is used in a specially prepared form.

The Society of Homeopaths

11 Brookfield
Duncan Close
Moulton Park
Northampton
Northamtonshire NN3 6WL
0845 450 6611
www.homeopathy-soh.org
info@homeopathy-soh.org
The SOH promotes public awareness of homeopathy, and maintains standards of practice and education. You can find local practitioners on the website.

The UK Homeopathic Medical Association

6 Livingstone Road
Gravesend
Kent DA12 5DZ
01474 560336
www.homoeopathy.org
info@the-hma.org
The UK HMA represents qualified professional homeopaths, and promotes homeopathy and homeopathic education. You can find a list of members on the website.

Kinesiology

Kinesiology is used to identify imbalances that could cause health problems. Kinesiology uses gentle muscle testing to isolate imbalances and corrections are made with gentle massage, energy work, Bach flower remedies and nutrition. It can help increase energy and vitality, prevent illness, improve posture, relieve physical pain and tension and help people to manage emotions and stress.

Kinesiology Federation
PO Box 28908
Dalkeith
EH22 2YQ
0870 011 3545
www.kinesiologyfederation.org
kfadmin@kinesiologyfederation.org
The Federation is a professional unifying organisation linking branches of kinesiology and the needs of the public. You can find local practitioners on the website.

Massage

Massage therapy treatment can help to improve and maintain a good posture increasing awareness of the whole body and improving emotional awareness. As wellas providing relaxation, massage also promotes better sleep, boosts immune system, improves skin condition and blood circulation, helps digestion and helps waste elimination.

International Association of Infant Massage
UK Chapter
40 Silk Mill Road
Redbourn
Hertfordshire AL3 7GE
01582 791933
www.iaim.org.uk
mail@iaim.org.uk
The purpose of the International Association of Infant Massage is to promote nurturing touch and communication through training, education and research.

General Council for Massage Therapy
46 Millmead Way
Hertford
Hertfordshire SG14 3YH
01992 537637
www.gcmt-uk.org
admin@gcmt-uk.org
The GCMT is the leading body for the promotion, regulation and research of massage therapy in the UK..

Naturopathy

Naturopathy is an approach to health care which aims to promote, restore and maintain health. The following principles underpin the practise of naturopathy: the healing power of nature, connection and interaction between the structural, biochemical and mental/emotional components of all living beings and the uniqueness of the individual. Some of the methods used may include clinical dietetics and applied nutrition, detoxification techniques and hydrotherapy.

General Council and Register of Naturopaths
Goswell House
2 Goswell Road
Street
Somerset BA16 0JG
0870 745 6984
www.naturopathy.org.uk
admin@naturopathy.org.uk
The General Council and Register of Naturopaths provides information on naturopathy and maintains professional standards. Will also put you in touch with naturopaths in your area.

Osteopathy

Osteopathy is a system of diagnosis and treatment, which lays its main emphasis on the structural and functional integrity of the body. It recognises that much of the pain and disability which we suffer, stems from abnormalities in the function of the body structure as well as damage caused to it by disease. The cranial approach to osteopathy suggests that the compressive forces experienced during birth as a result of the passage through the pelvis and the tight fit in the birth canal can cause imbalance in a baby's system. Common problems in new-born babies like colic, sucking problems, glue ear and respiratory difficulties may benefit from cranial osteopathic care.

General Osteopathic Council

176 Tower Bridge Road
London SE1 3LU
020 7357 6655
www.osteopathy.org.uk
concerns@osteopathy.org.uk

The GEC maintains standards within the profession, issues codes of practice and offers an information service. You can find local practitioners on the website.

British Osteopathic Association

Langham House West
Luton
Bedfordshire LU1 2NA
01582 488455
www.osteopathy.org
enquiries@osteopathy.org

The BOA is the largest professional association for osteopaths in the UK and is committed to promoting the highest standards of osteopathic education and research. You can find local practitioners on the website.

Osteopathic Centre for Children

The School House
Woodbridge Street
London EC1R 0ND
020 7490 5510
www.occ.uk.com

OCC offers osteopathic treatment for children up to 18yrs for a wide range of conditions.

Cranio-Sacral Therapy Association

Monmouth House
27 Old Gloucester Street
London WC1N 3XX
0700 078 4735
www.craniosacral.co.uk
office@craniosacral.co.uk

CSTA provides support to practitioners and monitors ethics and standards. You can find local practitioners on the website.

Psychotherapy

Child psychotherapy helps with a wide variety of problems including emotional and behaviour disorders, tantrums, bedwetting and soiling, eating and sleeping difficulties, nightmares, poor school performance, jealousy, excessive shyness, unhappiness, difficulties with relationships, fears and phobias.

British Association of Psychotherapists

37 Mapesbury Road
London NW2 4HJ
020 8452 9823
www.bap-psychotherapy.org
mail@bap-psychotherapy.org

The BAP Consultation and Psychotherapy Centre for Children, Adolescents and Families offers assessment and treatment for emotional and behavioural problems that have not been helped by ordinary measures. You can find local therapists by contacting the association.

The British Confederation of Psychotherapists

West Hill House
6 Swains Lane
London N6 6QS
020 7267 3626
www.bcp.org.uk
mail@bcp.org.uk

The BCP is an association of institutions, which comprise psychoanalysts, analytical psychologists, psychoanalytic psychotherapists and child psychotherapists. You can find local therapists on the website.

British Association for Counselling and Psychotherapy

BACP House
35–37 Albert Street
Rugby
Warwickshire CV21 2SG
0870 443 5252
www.bacp.co.uk
bacp@bacp.co.uk

The British Association for Counselling and Psychotherapy works to promote and provide education and training for counsellors and psychotherapists working in either voluntary or professional settings. You can find local therapists on the website.

Reflexology

Reflexology is a complementary therapy that works on the feet or hands enabling the body to heal itself. Following illness, stress, injury or disease the body may be in a state of imbalance with vital energy pathways blocked, thus preventing the body from functioning effectively. Reflexology can be used to restore and maintain the body's natural equilibrium and encourage healing.

Association of Reflexologists

5-6 Fore Street
Taunton
Somerset TA1 1HX
www.aor.org.uk
info@aor.org.uk

The AOR is the awarding body for the Practitioner Certificate in Reflexology. You can find local practitioners on the website.

The British Reflexology Association

Administration Office
Monks Orchard
Whitbourne
Worcester
Worcestershire WR6 5RB
01886 821207
www.britreflex.co.uk
bra@britreflex.co.uk

The BRA is a representative body for reflexologists and for students training in the method. You can find local practitioners on the website.

Spiritual Healers

Healing is the channelling of energies by the healer to re-energise the patient to deal with illness or injury. Healing can help with the speed and extent of recovery from serious illness and major surgery and from the effects of treatments such as chemotherapy and radiation therapy. It complements conventional medicine.

The Confederation of Healing Organisations

The Red and White House
113 High Street
Berkampstead
Hertfordshire HP4 2DJ
01442 870660

cho-healing@virgin.net

The CHO is a registered charity whose objective is to make contact and distant healing available in NHS and private medicine, as a complement to services offered by doctors.

National Federation of Spiritual Healers (non-denominational)

Old Manor Farm Studio
Church Street
Sunbury on Thames
Middlesex TW16 6RG
0845 123 2777
www.nfsh.org.uk
office@nfsh.org.uk

The NFSH trains and supports its membership to give healing to all who request it. NFSH members give healing in private practice, healing centres, and when requested in hospitals and hospices.

LOCAL COMPLEMENTARY AND ALTERNATIVE THERAPISTS

Georgia Askew BSc Lic LCCH
Homeopath

132 Coleford Bridge Road
Mytchett
Surrey GU16 6DS
01252 513229

■ *Flexible hours Mon-Fri, low cost children's clinic Thu 12:30-17:00*
■ *First appointment for children under 12 yrs £30 (£20 at Thu clinic), thereafter £20 (£15 at Thu clinic), morning sickness consultation £10, birth kit hire and consultation £15*

Offers safe and effective treatment for pregnancy, babies and beyond. P

Jennifer Bain
Homeopath

Hatchgate Farm
Pennypot Lane
Chobham
Surrey GU24 8DL
01276 856186
07976 558055
w.bain@btclick.com

■ *Flexible opening hours during daytime*
■ *£45 for first consultation, £35 thereafter.*

P

Sarah Brogue Lic LCCH RSHom
Homeopath

Fairlands Medical Centre
Fairlands Avenue
Fairlands
Worplesdon
Guildford
Surrey GU3 3NA
01483 812070

■ *Wed 09:15–13:00, plus flexible hours at nearby clinic, low cost children's every 1st Wednesday of the month*
■ *First appointment £50 children over 1yr, £40 for under 1yr, thereafter £25*
Pre-conceptual care offered, specialise in children's cases. Play area and toys available.

Beverley Burrows
Kinesiologist
104 Hermitage Woods Crescent
St Johns
Woking
Surrey GU21 8UF
01483 472444
07969 345271
beverley@burrows7454.freeserve.co.uk
■ *Tue and Fri*
■ *Children £30 (session length according to age)*
Home visits offered.

Gareth C Butler DO & Associates
Osteopath
West Byfleet Health Centre
Madeira Road
West Byfleet
Surrey KT14 6DH
01932 345287
01753 850322 for appointments - main practice based in Windsor
■ *Wed and Fri in West Byfleet. (May change to Thu and Fri)*
■ *New child patients £35, follow up appointments £25*
Cranial osteopathy treatments, specialise in treating pregnant women in preparation for childbirth and check ups for newborn infants.

Crofton Healthcare Ltd
Osteopath
Wych Hill
Woking
Surrey GU22 0ES
01483 770529
www.croftonhealthcare.co.uk
janlawler@croftonhealthcare.co.uk
■ *Wed 08:30–18:00, Fri 08:30–18:00*
■ *£40 for initial consultation, £35 for follow up*
Cranial osteopathy, acupuncture, dietary and nutrition advice. Play area and toys available.

Emily Dillon
Osteopath
Westfield Osteopathic Practice
1 Westfield Road
Woking
Surrey GU22 9LZ
01483 768810
■ *Mon 08:00–16:00, Wed and Fri 08:00–20:00*
■ *£30 per visit*
Cranial osteopathy treatments. Parking shared with Dental Practice next door. Home visits offered.

Dr Econs MRCS LRCP
Allergist
Thames Allergy Centres
Woking Nuffield Hospital
Shores Road
Woking
Surrey GU21 2BY
Also at:
22 Barham Close
Weybridge
Surrey KT13 9PR
01932 703097
www.thamesallergy.com
thamesallergy@aol.com
■ *Mon-Fri 09:00-17:00*
■ *£105 for initial consultation, £60 for follow up*

Assessment and advice on maximising health for mother and baby during antenatal period and infancy. Emphasis on basic dietary changes and improving nutritional status. Conditions such as eczema, asthma, upper respiratory infections, food intolerance and colic treated. Home visits offered.

Robert Every BSc RSHom
Homeopath

Starlings
Wych Hill
Woking
Surrey GU22 0EU
01483 765288

■ *Mon-Fri 09:00–19:00, Sat 09:00-12:30*
■ *£35 per visit*

Offers natural childbirth remedies and other homeopathic treatment. Home visits offered. Play area and toys available.

Sonja Freebody IIHHT, VTCT Dip
Indian Head Massage Therapist

Gate House
Oak Grange Road
West Clandon
Surrey GU4 7TZ
01483 452900
07884 185090
andysonja@btopenworld.com

■ *Mon-Sun by appointment*
■ *£15 for full 25-30 minute treatment*

Indian head massage for ladies and children only. Massage to shoulders, upper arms, neck, head and face. Can help with relaxation, stress, head-aches, stiffness, sleep disorders. Home visits and groups sessions offered. Gift vouchers available. Play area.

Godalming Chiropractic Clinic
Chiropractor

Bridge Road
Godalming
Surrey GU7 3DT
01483 419538
www.godalmingclinic.co.uk

■ *Mon-Sat*
■ *£50 without x-rays (£70 with), £28 thereafter*

Wide range of services offered within the chiropractic scope of practice, including special interest in treatment of pregnant women and paediatrics.

Suzanne Hoddinott BSc (Hons), Ost.Med, DPO, DO, ND
Osteopath and Naturopath

Wishing Well Natural Health Clinic
Barn Cottage
Bonsey Lane
Westfield
Woking
Surrey GU22 9PP
01483 764582
07885 792178
www.abc-osteopath.co.uk

■ *Mon-Sat by appointment*
■ *£30 initial consultation (45 minutes), £25 thereafter for babies/children (30 minutes). £35 Mother & Baby (0-16 wks old) consultation (1 1/4 hours)*

Offers structural, cranial and paediatric osteopathy and naturopathy treatment for all age groups, all stages of pregnancy and post natal care. Play area with toys available.

Beth Ingham MBAcC
Acupuncturist

117 York Road
Woking
Surrey GU22 7XR
01483 715366

■ *Mon-Fri*
■ *£35 first consultation, £28 thereafter*
Offers treatment for asthma/eczema, headaches/migraine, morning sickness. Acupuncture to induce labour, teaching acupressure to pregnant patients and partners for use as pain relief during childbirth. Can also help with many female reproductive system disorders. Prefer to treat children and mothers of young children in their own homes. P

Joanna Kolker DO
Osteopath

The White House
Lavender Road
Woking
Surrey GU22 8AY
01483 755597

■ *Mon 09:30-18:00, Thu and Fri 09:30-18:30*
■ *£25 under 16yrs*
Offers structural and cranio-sacral technique osteopathy. Particular interest in treating ante/post natal mums. Post natal check ups recommended for babies. Treatment for colic, sleep disturbance, glue ear, learning/behavioural difficulties.
P

Lisa Lindsay DO
Osteopath, Naturopath, Cranial Osteopath

Calda
Wood Lane
Knaphill
Woking
Surrey GU21 2AD
01483 489501

■ *Open by appointment*
■ *£35 for first consultation and treatment, £32 thereafter*

Offers osteopathy for pregnancy, cranial osteopathy for feeding, sleeping difficulties, colic and naturopathy treatments. Home visits offered on emergency basis only. Play area.

Yvonne Longman MAR & Reiki Master
Reflexologist, Reiki, Indian Head Massage

5 Firwood Close
St Johns
Woking
Surrey GU21 8UQ
07770 484592
headandtoes@hotmail.com

■ *Mon-Sat by appointment*
■ *From £20 (concessions for children)*

Offers reflexology, reiki and Indian head massage to children, babies and adults, as well as Hopi Ear Candling from 5 yrs. Treatments include pre-conceptual care through to pregnancy, labour and post-natal care. NHS registered. Home visits offered. Pushchair and double buggy access to porch. **P**

Joy Marson
Nutritionist

Bulbeggars
Church Hill
Horsell
Woking
Surrey GU21 4QE
01483 763318

■ *Mon 09:00-17:00*
■ *£30 for initial consultation*

Treats problems relating to nutrition, allergies, eczema. Walking access only to treatment room. Home visits offered. **P**

New Haw Therapy Clinic
Osteopath, Chiropractic, Nutritionist, Homeopath, Massage and Aromatherapist

189 Woodham Lane
New Haw
Surrey KT15 3NN
01932 351120

■ *Mon-Thu 09:00-21:00, Fri 09:00-18:30, Sat 09:00-13:00*
■ *£38 for initial consultation, £32 thereafter*

Offers range of treatments, including cranial osteopathy suitable from birth and structural osteopathy suitable for ante & post natal problems, such as PSD and back ache. Free no-obligation discussion available if you wish to find out more about the therapies offered. **P**

Matthew Schrock DO(Hons), Cert.Ed.
Osteopath and Kinesiologist

17 Holyoake Avenue
Horsell
Woking
Surrey GU21 4PW
01483 756392
schrock@btinternet.com

■ *Tue-Thu*
■ *£45 per hour*

Specialises in working with children with learning difficulties and with ante/post-natal mums. Leaflets available on request. Offers home visits. **P**

Jo Sutton
Dietician

PO Box 780
Knaphill
Woking
Surrey GU21 2WA
01483 476905
www.atastefornutrition.com

■ *Mon-Fri 09:00–17:00*
■ *£82 for 1 1/2 hours, £65 for next 45 minutes then £45 for subsequent visits*
Works out of Guildford and Woking. Consultant dietician treating a wide range of illnesses, allergies and intolerances. Home visits offered. Free parking at Woking clinic.

Annie Williams RGN RM RHV MCH RSHom
Homeopath and Nutritionalist

The Holistic Centre
175,Send Road
Send
Woking
Surrey GU23 7ET
Also at:
Verstage House
Meadrow
Godalming
Surrey GU7 3HZ
01483 417330 for appointments

■ *Mon-Fri*
■ *£45 per hour*
Trained nurse, midwife and health visitor working as a homeopath and nutritionalist for the last 15 years. Home visits offered in emergencies.

HOSPITALS

Frimley Park Hospital

Portsmouth Road
Frimley
Surrey GU16 7UJ
Access via St. Peter's hospital website
www.ashfordstpeters.nhs.uk
Acute hospital with dedicated children's accident and emergency. Parking is pay and display but demand can be high in the afternoon.

Royal Surrey County Hospital

Egerton Road
Guildford
Surrey GU2 7XX
01483 571122
www.royalsurrey.nhs.uk
Acute hospital with accident and emergency.

St. Peter's Hospital

Guildford Road
Chertsey
Surrey KT16 0PZ
01932 872000
www.ashfordstpeters.nhs.uk
Acute hospital that is part of Ashford and St. Peter's NHS Trust. Has dedicated children's accident and emergency with play area. Parking is pay and display.

Weybridge Community Hospital

22 Church Street
Weybridge
Surrey KT13 8DY
01932 852931

■ *Walk in centre Mon-Fri 07:00-22:00, Sat-Sun 09:00-22:00*
Walk in centre for minor injuries and minor health ailments. Service is for adults and children over 2yrs. Pharmacy on site. Located in town centre. Parking is pay and display and can get very busy.

Woking Community Hospital

Heathside Road
Woking
Surrey GU22 7HS
01483 715911

■ *Walk in centre Mon-Fri 07:00-22:00, Sat-Sun 09:00-22:00*
Community hospital that is part of Woking Primary Care Trust. Has walk in centre that is nurse led. Service is

for adults and children over 2yrs. Includes x-ray facilities. Waiting area has play area with toys. Free parking but can get very busy. **P**

PHARMACIES

The NHS website has a service that will search for the nearest pharmacy to your postcode.
www.nhs.uk/root/localnhsservices
For urgent prescriptions or medications outside hours please phone Woking police station on 01483 761991 or the NHS Direct on 0845 46 47 for the emergency pharmacists details.

Boots the Chemist

1-9 Commercial Way
Woking
Surrey GU21 6YA
01483 761648

■ *Mon-Tue 08:35-18:00, Wed 09:00-18:00, Thu-Sat 08:35-18:00, Sun 11:00-17:00*
Dispensing Pharmacy. Parking in town centre car parks.

Bridge Chemist

153 Maybury Road
Woking
Surrey GU21 5JR
01483 760696

■ *Mon-Fri 09:00-19:00, Sat 09:00-13:00*
Dispensing Pharmacy. **P**

Kilnbridge Pharmacy

12 Hermitage Road
St Johns
Woking
Surrey GU21 8TB
01483 762241

■ *Mon-Fri 09:00-19:00, Sat 09:00-17:30*
Dispensing Pharmacy. **P**

L Rowland & Co (Retail) Ltd

3 Gosden Road
West End
Woking
Surrey GU24 9LH
01483 473714

■ *Mon-Sat 09:00-13:00, 14:15-17:30*
Dispensing Pharmacy. **P**

Lloyds Pharmacy

1 London House
25 High Street
Ripley
Woking
Surrey GU23 6AA
01483 225111
www.lloydspharmacy.com

■ *Mon-Fri 09:00-18:00, Sat 09:00-17:00*
Dispensing Pharmacy. **P**

Lloyds Pharmacy

18 Windsor Road
Chobham
Surrey GU24 8LA
01276 512324
www.lloydspharmacy.com

■ *Mon-Fri 09:00-13:00, 14:00-18:30, Sat 09:00-13:00*
Dispensing Pharmacy. **P**

Lloyds Pharmacy

8 Marshall Parade
Coldharbour Road
Pyrford
Surrey GU22 8SW
01932 343556
www.lloydspharmacy.com

■ *Mon-Fri 09:00-13:00, 14:00-17:30, Sat 09:00-13:00*
Dispensing Pharmacy. **P**

Lloyds Pharmacy

Kingfield Road
Woking
Surrey GU22 9EH
01483 760565

www.lloydspharmacy.com
■ *Mon-Fri 09:00-18:30, Sat 09:00-17:00*
Dispensing Pharmacy. Some parking available on road.

Lloyds Pharmacy
2 West Lodge
Station Approach
West Byfleet
Surrey
KT14 6NG
01932 345004
■ *Mon-Fri 08:30-19:00, Sat 09:00-17:30*
Dispensing Pharmacy. Car parking in nearby Pay & Display.

May & Thomson
51 Dartmouth Avenue
Sheerwater
Woking
Surrey GU21 5PE
01932 346186
■ *Mon-Fri 09:00-17:30, Sat 09:00-13:00*
Dispensing Pharmacy. **P**

Moss Pharmacy
11-13 The Broadway
Knaphill
Woking
Surrey GU21 2DR
01483 472328
www.mosspharmacy.co.uk
■ *Mon-Fri 09:00-18:00, Sat 09:00-17:30*
Dispensing Pharmacy. **P**

Moss Pharmacy
34 Guildford Road
Woking
Surrey GU22 7QQ
01483 770900
www.mosspharmacy.co.uk
■ *Mon-Sun 09:00-21:00*
Dispensing Pharmacy. **P**

Moss Pharmacy
8 Goldsworth Park Centre
Woking
Surrey GU21 3LG
01483 726383
www.mosspharmacy.co.uk
■ *Mon-Fri 09:00-18:30, Sat 09:00-17:30*
Dispensing Pharmacy. **P**

Moss Pharmacy
91 High Street
Horsell
Woking
Surrey GU21 4SY
01483 772494
www.mosspharmacy.co.uk
■ *Mon-Sat 09:00-13:00, 14:00-17:30*
Dispensing Pharmacy. **P**

Moss Pharmacy
The Villages Medical Centre
Send Barnes Lane
Send
Woking
Surrey GU23 7BP
01483 222162
www.mosspharmacy.co.uk
■ *Mon 08:30-19:00,*
Tue-Fri 08:30-18:15, Sat 09:00-13:00
Dispensing Pharmacy. **P**

Moss Pharmacy
103 High Road
West Byfleet
Surrey KT14 7QX
01932 345284
www.mosspharmacy.co.uk
■ *Mon-Sat 09:00-17:30*
Dispensing Pharmacy. Pharmacist at lunch between 13:00-14:00. Parking in nearby car park.

The Parade Pharmacy
York House Medical Centre
Heathside Road
Woking
Surrey GU22 7XL
01483 714571

■ *Mon-Fri 08:30-18:30, Sat 09:00-12:30*
Dispensing Pharmacy. **P**

Tesco Instore Pharmacy

Barnes Wallace Drive
Brooklands
Weybridge
KT13 0XF
01932 747449

■ *Mon-Sat 09:00-20:00, Sun 10:00-16:00*
Non Dispensing Pharmacy. **P**

SUPPORT

BEREAVEMENT

Baby Mailing Preference Service

(part of Mailing Preference Service MPS)
DMA House
70 Margaret Street
London W1W 8SS
020 7291 3310 (General Enquiries)
www.mpsonline.org.uk
mps@dma.org.uk

Service is designed to help parents who have lost their baby and wish to avoid the hurt caused by company mail shots of baby products. By registering once with the Baby MPS, almost all unwanted mailing will be stopped. The information will be used only for this purpose and will be confidential.

British Organ Donor Society (BODY)

Balsham
Cambridge CB1 6DL
01223 893636
www.argonet.co.uk/body
body@argonet.co.uk

Run by parents of a donor to provide advice and counselling. You can obtain a Donor Registration Form with Donor Card appended by phoning 0845 60 60 400 (local call rate). Or you can join the NHS Organ Donor Register via the webpage www.uktransplant.org.uk

The Child Bereavement Trust

Aston House
West Wycombe
High Wycombe
Buckinghamshire HP14 3AG
01494 446648
0845 357 1000 (Helpline)
www.childbereavement.org.uk
enquiries@childbereavement.org.uk

Support line is part of a confidential service providing information, support and appropriate resources to professionals from all sectors caring for grieving families.

The Child Death Helpline

Child Death Helpline Department
Great Ormond Street Hospital
Great Ormond Street
London WC1N 3JH
020 7813 8551
0800 282 986 (Helpline)
www.childdeathhelpline.org

■ *Helpline 365 days 19:00-22:00, Mon-Fri 10:00-13:00, Wed 13:00-16:00*
Telephone support for all those affected by the death of a child.

The Compassionate Friends

53 North Street
Bristol
South Gloucestershire BS3 1EN
0117 966 5202
0845 123 2304 (Helpline)
www.tcf.org.uk
info@tcf.org.uk

■ *365 days 10:00–16:00, 18:30–22:30*
TCF is an organisation of bereaved parents and their families offering

understanding, support and encouragement to other parents, relatives and friends after the death of a child and to professionals helping the family.

The Cot Death Society

4 West Mills Yard
Kennet Road
Newbury
Berks RG14 5LP
01635 38137
0845 601 0234 (Monitor Helpline)
www.cotdeathsociety.org.uk
fundraising@cotdeathsociety.org.uk

The Society loans infant respiration monitors to families with babies who are at risk from cot death. These are provided, free of charge, upon medical referral.

CRUSE - Bereavement Care

126 Sheen Road
Richmond
Surrey TW9 1UR
0870 167 1677 (Helpline)
www.crusebereavementcare.org.uk
helpline@crusebereavementcare.org.uk

Anyone can contact Cruse if they want to talk about themselves or someone they know who has been affected by a death.

Daisy's Dream

PO Box 4738
Twyford
Reading
Berkshire RG10 9GT
0118 934 2604
info@daisysdream.org.uk
www.daisysdream.org.uk

Daisy's dream offers support for bereaved children and their families in Berkshire and the immediate surrounding area within Surrey.

Foundation for the Study of Infant Deaths

Artillery House
11–19 Artillery Row
London SW1P 1RT
0870 787 0554 (Helpline)
www.sids.org.uk/fsid
fsid@sids.org.uk

■ *Mon–Fri 09:00–23:00, Sat–Sun 18:00–23:00*

FSID is one of the UK's leading baby charities. FSID carries out its aims by funding research, supporting bereaved families and providing information on how to reduce the risk of cot death to health professionals and the public.

The Miscarriage Association

c/o Clayton Hospital
Northgate
Wakefield
West Yorkshire WF1 3JS
01924 200799 (Helpline)
www.miscarriageassociation.org.uk
info@miscarriageassociation.org.uk

■ *Mon–Fri 09:00–16:00*

Offers support and information, via website, leaflets and factsheets, telephone helpline and local support groups, for those suffering the effects of pregnancy loss.

Stillbirth and Neonatal Death Society

28 Portland Place
London W1B 1LY
020 7436 5881 (Helpline)

■ *Mon–Fri 10:00–15:00, with answerphone out of hours*

www.uk-sands.org
support@uk-sands.org

SANDS offers support for parents and families whose baby is stillborn or dies soon after birth through a national helpline, local support groups and "befrienders".

Winston's Wish (for bereaved children)

Clara Burgess Centre
Bayshill Road
Cheltenham
Gloucestershire GL50 3AW
0845 203 0405 (Helpline)
www.winstonswish.org.uk

Winston's Wish provides support for bereaved children and young people up to the age of 18.

CLASSES FOR PARENTS

Behaviour Clinics

St Johns Health Centre
Hermitage Road
St Johns
Woking
Surrey GU21 1TD
01483 764871

5/6 week courses during the day with a crèche, run by Health Visitors.

British Red Cross

Surrey Branch
Woodlands Road
Slyfield Green
Guildford
Surrey GU1 1RL
01483 300891
www.redcross.org.uk

Provide first aid training.

Family Caring Trust

8 Ashtree Enterprise Park
Newry
Co Down BT34 1BY
028 3026 4174
www.familycaring.co.uk
office@familycaring.co.uk
Woking contact Ann Mather 01483 730749

Family Caring Trust is a Charity founded in 1986 to support and empower parents by providing practical, skill-based resources to improve family relationships.

International Association of Infant Massage

IAIM UK Chapter
PO Box 247
Rainham
Essex RM13 7WJ
07816 289788
www.iaim.org.uk
mail@iaim.org.uk

■ *Mon-Tue 09:00-13:00 Thu-Fri 09:00-13:00*

Promoting nurturing touch and communication through training, education and research.

NCT Postnatal Course

Horsell
07005 801057

■ *10:15- 11:30, days to be arranged*

6 week course, for parents of babies up to 6mths old, covering topics such as coping with a crying baby, sleeping, safety at home, finding support and information, returning to work and making time for mum. The course may complement, but is not designed to replace or duplicate any NHS courses offered. The NCT Branch Library will be available to all course members.

Parenting Course

Holy Trinity Church
Chobham Road
Knaphill
Woking
Surrey GU21 2SY
01483 473489

■ *Wed 20:00*

8 week parenting course for parents of young children up to age of 6yrs. The course is designed to give parents a chance to stand back and with the support of other parents, find new

ways to nurture their children and become happier parents.

Postnatal Groups

01483 764871 St Johns Health Centre
01483 715911 Woking Community Hospital
01932 340411 West Byfleet Health Centre
01483 728201 Goldsworth Park Health Centre

Health Visitors Secretary is the contact in each case
Run by health visitors, this 6 week course, for parents of babies up to about 6mths old, covers topics such as coping with a crying baby, sleeping, first aid and safety at home, weaning and playing. Details can also be found at your GP surgery, or Child Health Clinic.

Practical Parenting

01483 730749

Fun and informal courses designed to help parents get on better with their children and increase their confidence in their own abilities as parents. Most daytime courses have free crèche. Pre-school courses available in Guildford, Woking, Chobham and other local areas.

Safe and Sound

60 Normandy Avenue
Barnet EN5 2JA
020 8449 8722
www.safe-and-sound.org.uk
info@safe-and-sound.org.uk

Safe and Sound run child safety and first aid courses for parents, au pairs, nannies and child carers. Courses run in the evenings in London area e.g. Wimbledon.

St. John Ambulance

Surrey Branch
St .John House
Stocton Close
Guildford
Surrey GU1 1HA
01483 450000

www.surrey.sja.org.uk

Provide first aid courses specifically designed for young children and babies.

Sunrise Group

Room D
Chertsey Hall
Heriot Road
Chertsey
Surrey KT16 9BX
Alison Fields 07870 858898

■ *Wed 10:00-12:00*
■ *Cost - free*

Social support group for young parents up to the age of 25. Organised events, trips, skills training and talks. Can take children to group, but focus of group is on the parents, rather than the child. Access for double buggies may be limited. Free parking limited, pay and display parking available. **P**

Woking Young Parents Group

Lakers Youth Centre
Denton Way
Goldsworth Park
Woking
Surrey GU21 3LP
Jessica Griffiths 07968 832397
Faye Stoneman 01483 727253

■ *Wed 13:00-15:00*
■ *Cost - free*

Social support group for young mums up to the age of 21. Organised events, trips, talks and skills training leading to nationally recognised qualifications. Can take children to group, but focus of group is on the parents, rather than the child. Transport provided on request. **P**

EARLY LEARNING

Bookstart

Book Trust
45 East Hill
London SW18 2QZ
020 8516 2977

www.bookstart.co.uk

National scheme offering free books to every child and advice to every parent. Parents usually receive the free Bookstart pack from the health visitor at the baby's 7-9 month developmental test.

North Surrey Local Education Office

Alexander House
55a-61a Commercial Way
Woking
Surrey GU21 6HN
01483 518120

Local office for education welfare issues.

Pre-School Learning Alliance (South East Region)

1st Floor
Sandon House
55 Quarry Hill
Tonbridge
Kent TN9 2SA
01732 363070

www.pre-school.org.uk

The Pre-school Learning Alliance works to support pre-schools across the whole of England.

Surrey County Council Education Website

www.surreycc.gov.uk/education

LOCAL GENERAL INFORMATION

Child Support
PO Box 55
Brierley Hill
West Midlands DY5 1YL
0845 713 3133
■ *Mon-Fri 08:00-20:00, Sat 09:00-17:00*

Citizen's Advice Bureau
Provincial house
26 Commercial Way
Woking
Surrey GU21 6EN
0845 120 2919
www.nacab.org.uk
www.wokingcab.org.uk
■ *Mon 10:00-16:00, Tue 10:00-19:00, Wed-Fri 10:00-16:00*
Offers free, confidential, impartial and independent advice related to debt and consumer issues, benefits, housing, legal matters and immigration. Wheelchair access to bureau, toilet and interview room.

Department of Health
Richmond House
79 Whitehall
London SW1A 2NL
020 7210 4850
www.doh.gov.uk
Provides health and social care policy, guidance and publications.

Department of Social Security
020 7712 2171
www.dss.gov.uk

DISS (Disability Information Service Surrey)
Harrowlands
Harrowlands Park
Dorking
Surrey RH4 2RA
www.diss.org.uk
National database of disability information.

North Surrey Primary Care Trust
Bournewood House
Guildford Road
Chertsey
Surrey KT16 0QA
01932 872010
www.nsurreypct.nhs.uk
website.feedback@nsurreypct.nhs.uk
Responsible for planning and securing health services and improving health of population in North Surrey area.

Police
Divisional Headquarters
Station Approach
Woking
Surrey GU22 7SY
0845 125 2222 (Surrey police switchboard - to report something)
www.surreypolice.uk

Registrar of Births, Deaths and Marriages (North Surrey)
Rylston
81 Oatlands Drive
Weybridge
Surrey KT13 9LN
01932 254369

Registrar of Births, Deaths and Marriages (West Surrey)
Artington House
Portsmouth Road
Guildford
Surrey GU2 5DZ
01483 562841

Social Services

West Surrey Assessment Team
Trizancia House
74 Chertsey Road
Woking
Surrey GU21 5BJ
01483 518484

Surrey Children's Information Service

0845 600 9009
■ *Mon-Fri 08:00-18:00*
surrey.cis@surreycc.gov.uk
Surrey Children's Information Service can provide information and advice on choosing and paying for early years and childcare, working with children, setting up your own childcare service, training, funding, nursery education grant, special needs, business and other support, childcare for your employees.

Surrey County Council

Contact centre
Room G33
County Hall
Penrhyn Road
Kingston upon Thames
Surrey KT1 2DN
0845 600 9009
■ *Mon-Fri 08:00-18:00*
www.surreycc.gov.uk
Main contact point for SCC for information on education including school places, the childrens information service (see above), roads and highways, disabled badges and jobs, or university funding and general info.

Visitor Information Centre

Crown House
Crown Square
Woking
Surrey GU21 6HR
01483 720103
www.woking.gov.uk/woking
tourist@woking.gov.uk
■ *Mon-Sat 09:00-17:00*
Oct-Mar: Mon-Fri 09:00-17:00,
Sat 09:00-16:00
Provides a wealth of information on Woking.

Woking Area Primary Care Trust

Woking Community Hospital
Heathside Road
Woking
Surrey GU22 7HS
01483 715911
www.woking.nhs.uk
Responsible for planning and securing health services and improving health of population in Woking area. Covers all wards in Woking Borough Council and Surrey Heath Borough Council.

Woking Borough Council

Gloucester Square
Woking
Surrey GU21 6YL
01483 755855
www.woking.gov.uk
■ *Mon-Fri 09:00-16:45*

Woking Twins Club

Catherine Burnham
01483 825693
cedgar@hotmail.com
Support group for parents of twins and multiple births of all ages. The Twins Club organises all kinds of events and runs a toddler group (see Local Activities section).

LOCAL SUPPORT FOR CHILDREN WITH SPECIAL NEEDS

Challengers
Stoke park
London Road
Guildford
Surrey GU1 1TU
01483 579390
www.disability-challengers.org

Provide play and leisure activities for disabled children including parent and toddler sessions, sibling groups and family days.

Cherry Trees
School Lane
East Clandon
Guildford
Surrey GU4 7RS
01483 222506
www.cherry-trees.co.uk

Provide short term respite care for children who have learning disabilities and/or physical disabilities.

Children's Challenge Group
New Horizons
4a Board School Road
Woking
Surrey GU21 5HE

Group offering therapy input to pre-school children with Special Needs. Referral usually via Health Visitor.

Early Bird
01932 563460 (for leaflet and information pack)
01737 737979 (queries)

Project that supports parents of children who have a diagnosis on the autistic spectrum. Early intervention program involving group training and individual sessions.

Link Leisure
New Horizons
4a Board School Road
Woking
Surrey GU21 5HE
01483 770037

Offer leisure and recreational activities to people with learning difficulties. From 4yrs upwards.

Partnership with Parents
Furzefield Primary School
Delabole Road
Merstham
Surrey RH1 3PA
01737 737300
www.pwp.surrey.org

Aims to ensure parents are able to play an informed part in any decision about the educational provision made to meet their son or daughter's Special Educational Needs by providing information, advice and support from pre-school to school leaving.

Rocking Horse RDA (Riding for the Disabled)
1 Shey Copse
Woking
Surrey GU22 8HS
01932 343571
www.riding-for-disabled.org.uk
rdahq@riding-for-disabled.org.uk

Offers riding facilities for the disabled.

Sheltered Swimming in Woking
Pool in the Park
01483 874611 Wendy Plues

■ *Fri 19:45-21:00*

All areas of pool open for people of all ages with physical or learning difficulties, over 60's, pregnant ladies and all special needs. Hoist and help available. Transport can be arranged.

Surrey Portage Service

South East Area Education Office
Omnibus Lesbourne Road
Reigate RH2 7JA
01737 737979
www.portage.org.uk

Home visiting educational service for pre-school children with additional support needs and their families. Can also contact Local Education Office.

White Lodge Centre

Holloway Hill
Chertsey
Surrey KT16 0AE
01932 567131
www.whitelodgecentre.co.uk

Resource which seeks to support disabled children and adults and their families/carers in the Surrey area by providing a range of flexible, creative and integrated services. Children's centre open 08:30-16:30 and includes the assessment, therapeutic treatment and pre-school education of children with cerebral palsy and like conditions. Family support services include care in child's home, overnight or day care. Also a toy library for families whose members include children with disabilities.

WIDE (Woking Information for Disability Enquiries)

Provincial House
26 Commercial Way
Woking
Surrey GU21 1EN
01483 747400
www.askwide.org.uk
info@askwide.org.uk

Free confidential information service open to anyone with a disability, their carers, friends, professionals or anyone with an interest in disability.

Woking Shop Mobility

The Peacocks
Level 1
Woking
Surrey GU21 6GD
01483 776612
www.wokingshopmobility.co.uk

■ *Mon-Fri 09:30-17:00, Sat 09:00-17:00*

Provide manual and powered wheelchairs and scooters to anyone with a mobility problem for a small charge.

NATIONAL SUPPORT ORGANISATIONS

Action for Blind People

14-16 Verney Road
London SE16 3DZ
0800 915 4666 (Helpline)
www.afbp.org
info@afbp.org

Action for blind people provides information, support and advice to those affected by a visual impairment, to help them make the most of their life and get the chances they deserve.

Action for Sick Children

c/o National Children's Bureau
8 Wakley Street
London EC1V 7QE
0800 074 4519
www.actionforsickchildren.org

Action for Sick Children offers advice if you have a problem or query regarding your child's healthcare, from how to register your child with a GP, to what to expect when they go into hospital.

Afasic

2nd Floor
50-52 Great Sutton Street
London EC1V 0DJ
0845 355 5577 (Helpline)

■ *Mon-Fri 11:00-14:00*
www.afasic.org.uk
info@afasic.org.uk
Afasic provides information and support for the families of children and young people with speech and language impairments.

Association for Spina Bifida and Hydrocephalus (ASBAH)

42 Park Road
Peterborough
Cambridgeshire PE1 2UQ
01733 555988
www.asbah.org
info@asbah.org
ASBAH offers information, advice and local support to people affected by spina bifida and/or hydrocephalus.

Birth Defects Foundation (BDF)

BDF Centre
Hemlock Business Park
Hemlock Way
Cannock
Staffordshire WS11 7GF
0870 070 7020 (Helpline)
■ *Mon-Fri 09:30-19:00, Sat 09:30–17:00*
www.birthdefects.co.uk
enquiries@birthdefects.co.uk
BDF offers information, advice and support to those affected by a birth defect.

BLISS

68 South Lambeth Road
London SW8 1RL
0500 618 140 (Helpline)
■ *Mon-Fri 10:00-17:00*
www.bliss.org.uk
information@bliss.org.uk
BLISS offers information, advice and support to the families of premature babies.

British Allergy Foundation

Allergy UK
Deepdene House
30 Bellegrove Road
Welling
Kent DA16 3PY
020 8303 8583 (Allergy Helpline)
020 8303 8525 (Chemical Sensitivity Helpline)
www.allergyfoundation.com
info@allergyuk.org
■ *Allergy Helpline Mon-Fri 09:00-21:00*
Chemical Sensitivity Helpline Mon-Fri 09:00-17:00
Allergy UK provides up to date information, advice and support to help you with your allergy.

British Stammering Association (BSA)

15 Old Ford Road
London E2 9JP
0845 603 2001 (Helpline)
www.stammering.org
info@stammering.org
The BSA helpline is a confidential service offering those affected by stammering, information, support and contact details for your local NHS speech and language therapy service.

British Dental Health Foundation

Smile House
2 East Union Street
Rugby
Warwickshire CV22 6AJ
0845 063 1188 (Dental Helpline)
■ *Mon-Fri 09:00-17:00*
www.dentalhealth.org.uk
mail@dentalhealth.org.uk
The British Dental Health Foundation provides information and advice on oral health matters.

British Diabetic Association
10 Parkway
London NW1 7AA
0845 120 2960 (Helpline)
■ *Mon-Fri 09:00-17:00 recorded info at other times*
www.diabetes.org.uk
info@diabetes.org.uk
The British Diabetic Association offers information, advice and local support to those affected by diabetes.

British Dyslexia Association
98 London Road
Reading
Berkshire RG1 5AU
0118 966 8271 (Helpline)
www.bda-dyslexia.org.uk
info@bda-dyslexia.demon.co.uk
The British Dyslexia Association gives information, advice and support to the dyslexic community.

British Epilepsy Association
New Anstey House
Gate Way Drive
Yeadon
Leeds
West Yorkshire LS19 7XY
0808 800 5050 (Helpline)
www.epilepsy.org.uk
helpline@epilepsy.org.uk
The BEA offers information, advice and support to all those affected by epilepsy.

British Institute for Brain Injured Children (BIBIC)
Knowle Hall
Bridgwater
Somerset TA7 8PJ
01278 684060
www.bibic.co.uk
BIBIC helps children with a learning difficulty reach their full potential and live a fulfilling and personally more rewarding life.

Cancer and Leukemia in Childhood (CLIC)
Abbey Wood Business Park
Filton
Bristol BS34 7JU
0845 301 0031
www.clic.org.uk
info@clic.org.uk
CLIC recognises the extreme pressures placed on families when a child is diagnosed with cancer or leukemia and works towards meeting the clinical, practical, financial and emotional needs of children and their families.

Changing Faces
1-2 Junction Mews
London W2 1PN
020 7706 4232
www.changingfaces.co.uk
info@changingfaces.co.uk
Changing Faces' primary focus is on disfigurements affecting the face, but much of their work has relevance to any disfigurement and disfiguring conditions, whatever the origin.

Child Accident Prevention Trust
18-20 Farringdon Lane
London EC1R 3HA
020 7608 3828
www.capt.org.uk
safe@capt.org.uk
The Child Accident Prevention Trust offers advice and information on the prevention of accidental injury.

Child Growth Foundation (CGF)
2 Mayfield Avenue
Chiswick
London W4 1PW
020 8995 0257
www.heightmatters.org.uk

CGF supports all persons (either children or adults) suffering from growth disorders and their families.

Children Living with Inherited Metabolic Diseases (CLIMB)

Climb Building
176 Nantwich Road
Crewe
Cheshire CW2 6BG
0800 652 3181 (Helpline – Parents and Professionals)
0870 770 0326 (Helpline - Childrens and Young persons Services)
www.climb.org.uk

CLIMB provides information, advice and support for children, young people and families affected by metabolic disease. CLIMB has formed the National Information and Advice Centre for Metabolic Diseases.

The Children's Society

Edward Rudolf House
Margery Street
London WC1X 0JL
0845 300 1128
www.the-childrens-society.org.uk
supporteraction@childrenssociety.org.uk

The Children's Society works with and for children to help them deal with life's harshest challenges and face the future with confidence.

Children's Liver Disease Foundation

36 Great Charles Street
Birmingham
West Midlands B3 3JY
0121 212 3839
www.childliverdisease.org
cldf@childliverdisease.org

The Children's Liver Disease Foundation supports all those affected by liver disease.

Cleft Lip and Palate Association (CLAPA)

Third Floor
235-237 Finchley Road
London NW3 6LS
020 7431 0033
www.clapa.com
info@clapa.com

CLAPA provides support for new parents, and for people with the condition and their families, from infancy through to adulthood.

Cystic Fibrosis Trust

11 London Road
Bromley
Kent BR1 1BY
020 8464 7211
www.cftrust.org.uk

The Cystic Fibrosis Trust aims to ensure that people with cystic fibrosis receive the best possible care and support in all aspects of their lives.

Disabled Living Foundation

380-384 Harrow Road
London W9 2HU
0845 130 9177 (Helpline)
www.dlf.org.uk
■ *Mon-Fri 10:00-13:00*

The Disabled Living Foundation works to support people with disabilities and provide information and advice on equipment and assistive technologies.

Down's Heart Group

17 Cantilupe Close
Eaton Bray
Dunstable
Bedfordshire LU6 2EA
01525 220379
www.downs-heart.downsnet.org
downs_heart_group@msn.com

The Down's Heart Group is a UK charity which offers information, advice and support to families who have a member with Down's Syndrome and congenital heart defects.

Down's Syndrome Association

Langdon Down Centre
2a Langdon Park
Teddington
Middlesex TW11 9PS
0845 230 0372
www.downs-syndrome.org.uk
info@downs-syndrome.org.uk

The Down's Syndrome Association helps people with Down's Syndrome to live full and rewarding lives.

Dyspraxia Foundation

8 West Alley
Hitchin
Hertfordshire SG5 1EG
www.dyspraxiafoundation.org.uk
admin@dyspraxiafoundation.org.uk

The Dyspraxia Foundation exists to help people understand and cope with dyspraxia. They provide information and local support groups.

The Enuresis Resource & Information Centre (ERIC)

34 Old School House
Britannia Road
Kingswood
Bristol BS15 8DB
0117 960 3060
www.enuresis.org.uk
info@eric.org.uk

The Enuresis Resource and Information Centre [ERIC] provides advice and information about the common and stressful condition of nocturnal enuresis or bedwetting. ERIC also offers advice on childhood day-time wetting and soiling.

The Eyecare Trust

PO Box 131
Market Rasen
Lincolnshire LN8 5TS
0845 129 5001
www.eyecare-information-service.org.uk
info@eyecaretrust.org.uk

The Eyecare Trust acts as an independant source of information on all eye-related issues.

Face to Face

Early Years Unit
Scope
42 St Owen Street
Hereford
Herefordshire HR1 2PR
01432 370860
www.face2facenetwork.org.uk
face2facenetwork@scope.org.uk

Support service for parents of children with Special Needs. There are local Surrey groups that offer one to one support.

Genetic Interest Group (GIG)

Unit 4d
Leroy House
436 Essex Road
London N1 3QP
020 7704 3141
www.gig.org.uk
post@gig.org.uk

The Genetic Interest Group (GIG) works to benefit all people affected by genetic disorders.

Haemophilia Society

Chesterfield House
385 Euston Road
London NW1 3AU
0800 018 6068 (Helpline)
www.haemophilia.org.uk
info@haemophilia.org.uk

The Haemophilia Society works to secure the best possible care, treatment and support for people with haemophilia or a related bleeding disorder and their families.

Hyperactive Children Support Group (HCSG)

71 Whyke Lane
Chichester
West Sussex PO19 7PD
01243 551313
www.hacsg.org.uk
hyperactive@hacsg.org.uk

The Hyperactive Children's Support Group helps and provides information for ADHD/Hyperactive children and their families.

I CAN

4 Dyer's Buildings
Holborn
London EC1N 2QP
0845 225 4071
www.ican.org.uk

I CAN helps children with speech and language difficulties, it works to create a society where their special needs are recognised, understood and met, so that they have the same opportunities in life as other children.

In Touch

10 Norman Road
Sale
Cheshire M33 3DF
0161 905 2440

In Touch provides information, advice and support for parents of children with Special Needs.

Mencap

123 Golden Lane
London EC1Y 0RT
0808 808 1111 (Helpline)
www.mencap.org.uk
help@mencap.org.uk

Mencap is a charity that works with people with learning disabilities, their families and carers.

Meningitis Research Foundation

Midland Way
Thornbury
Bristol
South Gloucestershire BS35 2BS
0808 800 3344 (Helpline)
www.meningitis.org

The Meningitis Research Foundation offers a 24hr helpline providing access to information, advice and support at any time.

The National Association for Gifted Children (NAGC)

Suite 14
Challenge House
Sherwood Drive
Bletchley
Milton Keynes MK3 6DP
0845 450 0221
www.nagcbritain.org.uk
amazingchildren@nagcbritain.org.uk

NAGC works to ensure that appropriate provision is made for children to develop their gifts and talents to the maximum.

The National Association for Special Educational Needs (NASEN)

NASEN House
4-5 Amber Business Village
Amber Close
Amington
Tamworth
Staffordshire B77 4RP
01827 311500
www.nasen.org.uk
welcome@nasen.org.uk

Through its local and national networks, teachers, parents, governors and other professionals can receive up-to-date information on Special Educational Needs provision and practice in the UK.

National Asthma Campaign

Providence House
Providence Place
London N1 0NT
0845 701 0203 (Helpline)
www.asthma.org.uk

The National Asthma Campaign offers independent help and advice to everyone affected by asthma.

National Autistic Society

The National Autistic Society
393 City Road
London EC1V 1NG
0870 600 85 85 (Helpline)
0845 070 4004 (Autism Helpline)
020 7903 3599 (Information Centre)
www.nas.org.uk
autismhelpline@nas.org.uk (Helpline)
info@nas.org.uk (Information Centre)

The National Autistic Society (NAS) Autism Helpline provides impartial confidential information, advice and support to people with autistic spectrum disorders, their families, and professionals.

The National Deaf Children's Society

15 Dufferin Street
London EC1Y 8UR
0808 800 8880 (Helpline)
www.ndcs.org.uk
ndcs@ndcs.org.uk
helpline@ndcs.org.uk

NDCS provides impartial information, advice and support on every aspect of childhood deafness. NDCS can help with welfare rights and benefit claims, making educational choices, advice on health, audiology and technology.

National Eczema Society

Hill House
Highgate Hill
London N19 5NA
0870 241 3604 (Helpline Mon-Fri 08:00-20:00)
www.eczema.org
helpline@eczema.org

The National Eczema Society provides information on a wide range of eczema related subjects.

National Meningitis Trust

Fern House
Bath Road
Stroud
Gloucestershire GL5 3TJ
0845 600 0800 (Helpline)
www.meningitis-trust.org
info@meningitis-trust.org
helpline@meningitis-trust.org

The National Meningitis Trust provides support to people affected by meningitis and septicaemia, through a range of professional services.

Reach – The Association for Children with Hand or Arm Deficiency

PO Box 54
Helston
Cornwall TR13 8WD
0845 130 6225
www.reach.org.uk
reach@reach.org.uk

Reach provides information, advice and support for children with hand or arm deficiencies and their parents.

Royal National Institute of the Blind

105 Judd Street
London WC1H 9NE

0845 766 9999 (Helpline)
www.rnib.org.uk
helpline@rnib.org.uk
■ *Mon-Fri 09:00-17:00*
The RNIB offers support, information and advice to all those affected by sight problems.

Royal National Institute of the Deaf

19-23 Featherstone Street
London EC1Y 8SL
0808 808 0123 (Helpline)
0808 808 6666 (Tinnitus Helpline)
www.rnid.org.uk
informationline@rnid.org.uk
tinnitushelpline@rnid.org.uk
The RNID offers support, information and advice to all those affected by hearing problems

SAVI – Surrey Association for Visual Impairment

Rentwood
School Lane
Fetcham
Surrey KT22 9JX
01372 377701
www.surreywebsight.org.uk
SAVI works with blind and partially sighted people, to provide services, equipment and advice, so that they may lead fuller, more independent lives.

SCOPE

PO Box 833
Milton Keynes
Buckinghamshire MK12 5NY
0808 800 3333 (Helpline)
www.scope.org.uk
cphelpline@scope.org.uk
■ *Mon-Fri 09:00-21:00, Sat-Sun 14:00-18:00 answerphone out of hours*
SCOPE provides information, advice and support to those affected by cerebral palsy.

Shooting Star Hospice for Children

Kathryn House
The Mews
53 High Street
Hampton Hill
Middlesex TW12 1ND
020 8481 8180
info@shootingstar.org.uk
www.shootingstar.org.uk
The Shooting Star Trust helps children in the western half of London and north Surrey who are not expected to live beyond early adulthood.

Sickle Cell Society

54 Station Road
London NW10 4UA
020 8961 7795
www.sicklecellsociety.org
info@sicklecellsociety.org
The Sickle Cell Society provides information, counselling and care for those with Sickle Cell Disorders and their families

TAMBA - Twins and Multiple Birth Association

2 The Willows
Gardner Road
Guildford
Surrey GU1 4PG
0800 138 0509 (Twinline)
■ *Mon-Fri 10:00-13:00, 19:00-22:00, Sat-Sun 10:00-22:00*
www.tamba.org.uk
enquiries@tamba.org.uk
TAMBA provides information and mutual support networks for families of twins, triplets and more, highlighting their unique needs to all involved in their care.

YoungMinds

102-108 Clerkenwell Road
London EC1M 5SA
0800 018 2138 (Parent's Information Service)

www.youngminds.org.uk

YoungMinds works to promote the mental health of children and young people. The Helpline provides free information and advice for any adult with concerns about the mental health of a child or young person.

PARENTING AND FAMILY SUPPORT

Contact A Family

209-211 City Road
London EC1V 1JN
020 7608 8700
0808 808 3555 (Helpline)
www.cafamily.org.uk
info@cafamily.org.uk

■ *Helpline Mon-Fri 10:00-16:00*

Contact a family provides information, support and advice for families with disabled children.

Family Crisis Line

01483 722533 (Helpline)

■ *Sun-Fri 10:00-17:30, 20:00-22:00, not bank holidays*

A group that provides information, support and advice for those with family difficulties.

Family Line Surrey

0808 800 5678

Freephone helpline offering listening and support to parents and families. Can provide information on groups and services for families in Surrey.

Families Need Fathers (FNF)

134 Curtain Road
London EC2A 3AR
0870 760 7496 (Helpline)
www.fnf.org.uk

Families Need Fathers provides information, support and advice to parents, including unmarried parents, of either sex. FNF is chiefly concerned with the problems of maintaining a child's relationship with both parents during and after family breakdown.

Fathers Direct

Herald House
Lambs Passage
Bunhill Row
London EC1Y 8TQ
020 7920 9491
www.fathersdirect.com

Fathers Direct is the UK's national information centre for fatherhood. It exists to support the welfare of children by the positive and active involvement of fathers and male carers in their lives.

Gingerbread

7 Sovereign Close
Sovereign Court
London E1W 2HW
0800 018 4318 (Helpline Mon-Fri 09:00-17:00)
www.gingerbread.org.uk
advice@gingerbread.org.uk

Gingerbread provides information, support and advice to lone parent families.

Homestart

2 Salisbury Road
Leicester
Leicestershire LE1 7QR
0800 068 6368 (Helpline)
www.homestart.org.uk
info@home-start.org.uk

Homestart is a family support organization. Homestart volunteers visit families regularly in their own homes, usually once a week for between two and four hours. The visits are flexible and the volunteer and family together decide when the visits should take place and how the time will be spent.

Kidscape

2 Grosvenor Gardens
London SW1W 0DH
0845 120 5204 (Helpline)
www.kidscape.org.uk

■ *Mon-Fri 10:00-16:00*

Kidscape works to prevent bullying and child sexual abuse. They offer information, support and advice to parents and their children.

National Council for One Parent Families

255 Kentish Town Road
London NW5 2LX
0800 018 5026 (Lone Parent Helpline)
www.oneparentfamilies.org.uk
info@oneparentfamilies.org.uk

One Parent Families provides information for lone parents on a variety of issues including: maintenance, tax credits, benefits, work, education, legal rights, childcare and holidays. Also information about other organisations and local groups who may be able to help.

Parentline Plus

0808 800 2222
www.parentlineplus.org.uk

Free and confidential helpline for anyone looking after a child.

Positive Parenting

2a South Street
Gosport
Hampshire PO12 1ES
023 9252 8787
www.parenting.org.uk
info@parenting.org.uk

Positive Parenting provide information, resources and training courses for parents.

Single Parent Action Network

Millpond
Baptist Street
Easton
Bristol BS5 0YW
0117 951 4231 (Helpline)
www.spanuk.org.uk
info@spanuk.org.uk

■ *Mon-Fri 09:30-12:30, 13:30-15:30*

Single Parent Action Network is a multi-racial organisation of single parents working to improve the lives of one parent families in the UK and Europe. They provide information, advice and local support.

Sure Start

Sure Start Unit
Department for Education and Skills and Department for Work and Pensions
Level 2
Caxton House
Tothill Street
London W1H 9NA
0870 000 2288
www.surestart.gov.uk
info.surestart@dfes.gsi.gov.uk

Sure Start is the Government's programme to deliver the best start in life for every child by bringing together early education, childcare and health and family support.

Surrey Women's Aid

01483 776822 (24hr helpline)
www.surreywomensaid.org.uk
help@surreywomensaid.org.uk

Support women and children experiencing domestic violence. Offer refuge, advice and support.

POSTNATAL SUPPORT

Association for Postnatal Depression

25 Jerdan Place
Fulham
London SW6 7EB
020 7386 0868 (Helpline)
www.apni.org

■ *Mon 10:00-14:00,*
Tue-Thu 10:00-17:00, Fri 10:00-14:00

Provides support to mothers suffering from postnatal depression & illness. Offers telephone helpline, information leaflets and network of volunteers.

Association of Breastfeeding Mothers

PO Box 207
Bridgwater
Somerset TA6 7YT
020 7813 1481 (Helpline)
www.abm.me.uk
info@abm.me.uk

Offers breastfeeding help, counselling, support groups, information and breast pumps.

Birth Reflections

St. Peter's Hospital
Guildford Road
Chertsey
Surrey KT16 0PZ
01932 722879

Gives parents opportunity to go through notes from birth experience and discuss any issues.

Breastfeeding Clinic

The Maybury Centre
27 Board School Road
Woking
Surrey GU21 5HD
07005 801057 or Wendy Deshpande
01483 715911 ext 6221

■ *Thu 09:45-11:30*

Support group run by Health Visitor and NCT Breastfeeding Counsellor to help mums with any breastfeeding problems. No appointments required.

Breastfeeding Counsellor (NCT)

0870 444 8708

For anyone who has concerns, before or after delivery, about feeding their baby, an NCT breastfeeding counsellor is available by telephone (sometimes in person). The counsellors are mothers who have breastfed their own babies and received specialist training in supporting others. You do not need to be an NCT member to take advantage of this service.

Connexions – Teenage Parents Personal Advisor

Diane Crew 01483 517070
www.surreycc.gov.uk

www.connexionssurrey.co.uk
diane.crew@surreycc.gov.uk

This part of the Connexions service offers information, advice, guidance and practical support for parents aged 13-19 in Surrey. Parents may be referred to this service by health or social care professionals or by self-referral.

Cry-sis

020 7404 5011 (Helpline)
www.cry-sis.com
info@cry-sis.org.uk
■ *Mon-Sun 09:00-22:00*

Offers support for families with excessively crying, sleepless or demanding babies.

La Leche League

0845 120 2918 (24hr Helpline)
www.laleche.org.uk

Helps mothers to breastfeed through mother to mother support, encouragement, information and education. Local support groups.

Listening Service – Royal Surrey County Hospital

07029 305149

Gives parents opportunity to go through notes from birth experience and discuss any issues. Leave a message on the answerphone and midwife will contact you.

Meet A Mum Association

Waterside Centre
25 Avenue Road
London SE25 4DX
020 8768 0123 (Helpline)
www.leuger.demon.co.uk
■ *Mon-Fri 19:00-22:00*

Help mothers who feel depressed and isolated when their babies are born. Offers local groups.

Postnatal Depression Support Counsellor (NCT)

01483 454789
www.postnataldepression.com
lwise@onetel.net.uk

Liz Wise is the UK specialist worker for the NCT in postnatal depression.

Postnatal Supporter (NCT)

07050 801057–Postnatal Co-ordinator

Woking Branch NCT can pair you up with another mother living near you who can offer practical assistance or reassurance. You do not need to be an NCT member to take advantage of this service.

SCBU – Transport Assistance (NCT)

07050 801057–SCBU Co-ordinator

Woking Branch NCT offers a voluntary service to drive mothers with transport difficulties to visit their babies in the Special Care Baby Unit at St Peters Hospital.

C

D

E

NCT membership application form

Application for membership

• Section 1

Membership of the National Childbirth Trust covers up to two people living at the same address.

I/we wish to beome a member of the National Childbirth Trust as indicated opposite. The National Childbirth Trust is a company limited by guarantee. I/we undertake that if, while I/we are a member or for one year thereafter, the company shall be wound up, I/we will continue to contribute to the assets of the company (in accordance with Clause 8 of its Memorandum) such sum as may be required not exceeding £1.00 ☐

(Please tick the type of membership you have chosen)

Standard membership (individual or couple)
First year £36, second & subsequent years £26
I/we wish to pay (please tick):

☐ Annually (cheque, card, direct debit)

☐ Quarterly direct debit – £9 per quarter (£6.50 second and subsequent years)

☐ Monthly direct debit – £3.50 per month (£2.50 second and subsequent years)

Reduced membership fee £1.00 per annum. Individuals or couples are eligible if they qualify for free NHS prescriptions (other than being pregnant/having a child under one). Qualifying groups are: Those in receipt of income support or income-based job seekers' allowance; recipients of working tax credit (which includes a disability element) or a tax credit with entitlement to an NHS credit exemption certificate ☐

Signature ______________________________
(please sign here if you qualify)

Four year and Ten year membership – Special inflation proof options.

Four years £100 ☐ Ten years £250 ☐

Donation to support the work of the NCT

£4 ☐ £9 ☐ £14 ☐ £ ______ (please specify)

INITIAL MEMBER

Surname ______________________________

Forename(s) ______________________________

Address ______________________________

______________________________ Postcode ______________

Telephone ______________________ Email ______________

Signature ______________________ Date ______________

SECOND MEMBER (if applicable)

Surname ______________________________

Forename(s) ______________________________

Signature ______________________ Date ______________

Which member will pay the membership fee? Name ______________________
(This allows us to claim the tax from the Inland Revenue, so please complete Section 2.)

I wish to join ______________ branch (if known, otherwise leave blank)

(Please fill in Section 2 overleaf if you are a taxpayer)
If you wish to pay either by cheque, CAF voucher of postal order please make it payable to The National Childbirth Trust and forward it with this completed form to the address given above. To pay be Direct Debit please go to Section 4 overleaf. To pay by Debit/Credit card please go to Section 3 overleaf.

Please tick box for free NCT book ☐

Join the easy way – if you have a credit/debit card phone 08709 90 80 40 now!

DIRECT Debit

The Direct Debit Guarantee This guarantee should be retained by the Payer.

- This Guarantee is offered by all Banks and Building Societies that take part in the Direct Debit Scheme. The efficiency and security of the Scheme is monitored and protected by your own Bank or Building Society.
- If the amounts to be paid or the payment rates change the NCT will notify you 14 working days in advance of your account being debited or as otherwise agreed.
- If an error is made by the NCT or your Bank or Building Society, you are guaranteed a full and immediate refund from your branch of the amount paid.
- You can cancel a Direct Debit at any time by writing to your Bank or Building Society. Please send a copy of your letter to us.

MF/07/xxxx

• Section 2 - Gift Aid

If you are a UK tax payer we will be able to recover tax paid by you, from the Inland Revenue on your membership fee and any donations you make to the NCT. At the basic rate of tax of 22% this means taht the work of the charity benefits by an additional £10 for instance, on the £36 membership fee – at no extra cost to you.

For joint members, if one member is a tax-payer, the tax paying partner should pay the membership fee and complete the Charitable Giving Dedaration below.

Charitable giving declaration

Name ______

Signed ______

Date ______

This dedaration confirms my wish to make a donation (including membership subscriptions) to The National Childbirth Trust under the Gift Aid scheme and applies to all donations/subscriptions made by me from 6th April 2000. I understand that I must pay an amount of Income Tax or Capital Gains Tax in the relevant tax year equal to any tax reclaimed by the NCT in that period. (Currently 28p for each £1 you give). I confirm that I am a UK tax payer, and that I will advise the NCT if this situation changes.

• Section 3 - Payment by Direct Debit

Instruction to your Bank or Building Society to pay by Direct Debit

DIRECT Debit

Please fill in this form, using a ballpoint pen.

Bank/Building Society ______

Address ______

______

______ Postcode ______

Name(s) of Account Holder ______

______

Branch Sort Code

Bank/Building Society Acc. No.

Originator's ID No. 7 7 0 5 5 2

Reference No. for NCT use only

Instruction to your Bank or Building Society: Please pay the National Childbirth Trust Direct Debits from the account detailed in this instruction subject to the safeguards assured by the Direct Debit Guarantee. I understand that this instruction may remain with the National Childbirth Trust and, if so, details will be passed electronically to my Bank/Building Society.

Signature(s) ______

Date ______

Banks and Building Societies may not accept Direct Debit Instructions for some type of accounts.

My preferred payment date is 3rd ☐ or 21st ☐ of the month

• Section 4 - Payment by credit/debit card

Please debit my Debit/Credit Card type ______ American Express not accepted

My membership fee to The National Childbirth Trust of £36/£100/£250/£1 (delete as applicable)

I wish to make an additional donation of £ ______ to the work of the NCT.

I understand that I may cancel this mandate at one week's notice and will be given a minimum of three weeks' notice of any change in the membership fee.

My card number is

Expiry Date

Issue No (Switch only)

Cardholders Name ______

Cardholders Address ______

______ Postcode ______

Authorised Signature ______ Date ______

The NCT will not sell your name and address to any other organisation. Your details will be held on our database so we can contact you with further information about the NCT and how you can support our work. However, from time to time we may undertake joint mailings with partner organisations. Please tick if you do not wish to receive further information ☐

MFAN/03/xxxx

When you have completed this form please mail it with your cheque or postal order, if applicable, to: MEMBERSHIP, The National Childbirth Trust, Alexandra House, Oldham Terrace, London W3 6NH. Please do not send cash.